In Loving Memory

of


Elizabeth Kent פיגא בת אהרון ז׳׳ל

Steve Kent ישראל יעקב בן קאפל הלוי ז׳׳ל

Linda Kent רבקה מאטל בת ישראל יעקב ז׳׳ל


Sarah Schwartz חיח שרה בת ר׳ משה ז׳׳ל

Milton Schwartz צבי מנחם מענדל בן מיכאל ז׳׳ל


Michael and Michelle Schwartz

and Family

# Conflict & Resolution in the Early Prophets

### Rabbi Allen Schwartz

KODESH PRESS

Conflict & Resolution in the Early Prophets
by Allen Schwartz

© Kodesh Press 2020

ISBN: 978-1-947857-34-6

Paperback Edition

Cover Design by Esti Schwartz

Text slightly revised July 2020

Distributed Exclusively by

Kodesh Press L.L.C.
New York, NY
www.kodeshpress.com
kodeshpress@gmail.com

The accounts in the early historical books of the Bible recount many incidents in which biblical figures appear to violate laws of the Torah and the narrator evinces no awareness of the violation. These passages have troubled traditional Jews through the ages. Rabbi Schwartz presents a thorough survey and explication of how the Rabbis of the Talmudic era confronted these questions supplemented by judicious selections from the resolutions proposed by later commentators. This is an enlightening work marked by erudition, clarity, and analytical precision.

— Dr. David Berger,
Dean of Bernard Revel Graduate School of Jewish Studies

Rabbi Allen Schwartz' *Conflict and Resolution in the Early Prophets* is a groundbreaking study that sheds significant light on how the Rabbis of the Talmud and Midrash understood Scripture. It is no secret that the plain sense of Scripture in the books of Joshua, Judges, and Samuel often presents cases of violation of Torah law by Israelites, with no condemnation of the perpetrators. Modern Bible scholarship simply assumes that Torah law was largely unknown in the period covered by the books of Joshua-Samuel. The Rabbis of the Talmud and Midrash thought otherwise, and the evidence for their understanding of Scripture is gathered together for the first time by Rabbi Schwartz. His lucid and erudite analysis of the rabbinic perspective will become the point of departure for all future discussion of this topic.

— Sid Z. Leiman,
Distinguished Professor of Jewish History and Literature,
Graduate School of Jewish Studies, Touro College;
Visiting Professor of Jewish History and Literature,
Bernard Revel Graduate School, Yeshiva University

Rabbi Schwartz's study is, to my knowledge, the first to deal in a systematic and methodical fashion with the question of how ostensible violations of biblical law are treated in rabbinic literature. His sophisticated taxonomy of rabbinic resolutions demonstrates the intensity with which the Sages viewed these activities and illustrates the lengths to which they went to render equitable judgment. Anyone who shares his reverence for the text and for the characters it portrays will welcome the fresh light it sheds on them and the new insights it provides into their behavior.

— Dr. Moshe Sokolow,
Associate Dean, Azrieli School of Jewish Education and Administration

# TABLE OF CONTENTS

# Preface

Rabbi Yechiel Epstein begins his colossal work, *Aruch ha-Shulchan*, with a description of the human conflict between our animalistic side and our angelic side. The heroes of the Bible serve as paradigms in assisting our angelic side to prevail in this conflict. Yet biblical heroes sometimes ran into their own conflicts. This does not in any way detract from their greatness, and moreover, makes them more accessible to us as paradigms, in our own struggles and in our own times of need.

The Psalmist lifts up his eyes to the mountains in his time of need, and our Sages draw a connection between the Hebrew word for "mountains" (*harim*) and the word for "parents" (*horim*). This work is dedicated in part to the memory of my mother, Chaya Sara bas Rav Moshe, *a"h*, and my father, Tzvi Menachem Mendel ben Michael, *a"h*. They built their lives from the ashes and taught us the values of self-sacrifice, the moral underpinnings and love of Torah, and Jewish observance. Their generation served as a crucial bridge of Jewish continuity at a very critical time for our people.

With an eye to the future, I thank my children, Shonnie, Chani, Moshe, Ellie, Esti, and Mindy for so many years of incredible *nachas*. They, their spouses, and our grandchildren are an everlasting source of joy.

This work would never have seen the light of day if not for the comments and significant technical contributions made by my life-partner, Alisa. Having typed this work originally on a Smith Corona typewriter for a Master's thesis at Bernard Revel Graduate School of Yeshiva University over 35 years ago, she repeated the feat for this publication. I express my gratitude to the professors of BRGS and the librarians at the Gottesman library of YU. It has been a pleasure to work with Alec Goldstein of Kodesh Press. His professionalism and work ethic are exemplary and there was never any conflict to be resolved.

Allen Schwartz
January 2020
New York, NY

# Introduction

This book has two major aims. First, it seeks to compile a list of apparent violations of Torah law embedded in the accounts recorded in the books of Joshua, Judges, and Samuel.[1] Violations that are recorded are all instances of flagrant disregard of the plain, literal sense of Torah law, where the perpetrator or narrator seems to be unaware of the fact that a violation has taken place. Such awareness requires explanation in the light of the biblical and rabbinic claims that the Torah was given publicly at Sinai prior to the events referred to in the books of Joshua, Judges, and Samuel. All characters in these books should therefore be aware of Torah law. If not the characters, then the narrator should have been aware of Torah law.[2] Violations of the law where they are recognized as such by either the perpetrator or the narrator are eliminated from this study, because it is clear that the perpetrator or narrator is aware of the wrongdoing.

---

1. The book of Kings is omitted from this study, except for four instances (1 Kings 3:4; 9:20-21; 18:20-24) where the violation in Kings has parallels in Joshua, Judges, or Samuel, and sheds light on our understanding of violations in the latter three books. This work was originally a Master of Arts thesis at Bernard Revel Graduate School of Yeshiva University under the guidance of Dr. Sidney Leiman, completed in 1985. An addendum to this study was added by Rabbi Meir Orlian, also as a Master's thesis at Bernard Revel, which similarly analyzes the book of Kings.

2. The Wellhausenian school, of course, resolves this problem with its contention that the earliest narrators of Joshua, Judges, and Samuel were unaware of the existence of Pentateuchal law in its present form. This work dismisses such a contention and shows that the Rabbis were well aware of these apparent omissions, and reacted to them.

For instance, David's violation of Torah law in his dealings with Bath-sheba (II Sam. 11) is not treated in this study because the perpetrator (ultimately) and the narrator indicate awareness of wrongdoing. Such awareness can be explained as reflecting knowledge of Torah law.

This list also includes instances in which a character in the books of Joshua, Judges, or Samuel seems to be ignorant of a Torah law without actually violating the law. For instance Samuel's anger at Israel's request for a king (I Sam. 8) implies ignorance of the Torah law to appoint a king (Deut. 17:12-20; see ch. 17). In addition, if a character intended to violate Torah law, his intentions are recorded here, even if he didn't actually violate the law. For instance, David's declaration that the stealer of sheep be killed (II Sam. 12:5) goes beyond the Torah's punishment for stealing sheep (Exod. 21:37), thus implying unawareness of Torah law (see ch. 37).

Second, this book will present the various rabbinic resolutions suggested in the Talmud and Midrash to these instances of flagrant violation of Torah law. "Rabbinic resolutions," as defined here, refer to all rabbinic material prior to the Geonic period. These resolutions lie scattered throughout rabbinic literature, and this work seeks to collect, classify, and analyze them.

Previous attempts to gather this material include Manasseh ben Israel's *Concilliator*, which lists a wide variety of textual inconsistencies and their resolutions. This list includes rabbinic reflection on some of the violations this study seeks to list. However, his reconciliations of the text do not offer an exhaustive collection of all the rabbinic resolutions. A preliminary attempt to classify some resolutions under the heading *hora'at sha'ah* was made by Z.H. Chajes.[3] According to this classification, the apparent violation of Torah law is an actual violation warranted by the situation at hand. A formal list of such examples appears also under the heading *hora'at*

---

3. Z.H. Chajes, *Kol Sifrei Maharitz Chajes*, vol. 1, pp. 23-43.

*sha'ah* in *Encyclopedia Talmudit*.[4] However, no one has gathered, classified, and analyzed all rabbinic resolutions to flagrant violations of Torah law in a systematic fashion. This work will be the first to attempt the task. Each chapter begins with a Torah law written under the heading "Torah." This is followed by the violation, or apparent or implied ignorance of that Torah law under the heading "Prophets." In the event that more than one example of violation is cited, each example will have a separate sub-heading. This is followed by an analysis of the rabbinic response.[5] The body of the study lists only rabbinic responses. The footnotes, however, include a selection of post-rabbinic resolutions of the violations. Doubtless there is room for a more exhaustive study of these violations from the standpoint of post-rabbinic commentaries. A recent work by Shimon Krasner, *Nahalat Shimon* [Hebrew], offers an exhaustive collection of rabbinic and post-rabbinic materials on issues in Joshua and Samuel. His work includes some of the issues raised here. A useful book regarding the rabbinic attitude toward wrongdoing on the part of different biblical characters is E. Margaliyot's *Ha-Hayyavim b'Mikra ve-Zakkaim b'Talmud u-v'Midrashim* [Hebrew]. One would expect to find justification for most of the apparent violations which are listed here. The prevailing rabbinic sentiment is that the reason why these apparent violations go unnoticed in the biblical narrative is that they are not really violations at all. Indeed the Rabbis often deny or explain away, not only violations which are unnoticed in the text, but also violations which <u>are</u> noticed by the text. For instance, David's actions with Bath-sheba are evil in the eyes of God (II Sam. 11:27), and David himself acknowledges the sinful nature of his actions (ibid. 12:13). Yet the Rabbis exonerate David of sin with Bath-sheba (BT *Shabbat* 56a; BT *Ketuvot* 9b). This is often the case with biblical characters who are considered righteous.

---

4. S.Y. Zevin, ed., *Encyclopedia Talmudit*, vol.8, columns 512-527.

5. If a resolution cannot be found for the violation at hand, sometimes another passage can, by analogy, serve as a resolution even though it doesn't directly address the problem. For example, see chapters 2 and 3.

The list of violations and their resolutions will be used in an attempt to shed more light on the approach of the Rabbis to wrongdoing in the Bible.[6]

The rabbinic resolutions to violations of Torah law can be categorized as follows:

## 1. Violation Denied

This is the most common category of rabbinic resolution to unnoticed violations. The resolution admits that one could mistakenly think that a violation has taken place. However, once the action of the biblical character is clarified, it becomes clear that no violation was committed. Therefore, of course, there was no awareness of violation in the biblical text.

A typical example of this category is the following case: Michal, after marrying David (I Sam. 18:27), was taken from him and given to Palti, son of Laish (ibid. 25:44). David subsequently took Michal back as his own wife after becoming king (I Sam. 3:14-15). No mention is made of the blatant disregard of the law of adultery on the parts of Michal and Palti, and even if David divorced Michal prior to her marriage to Palti, the text is silent regarding David's violation of the law forbidding a man to remarry a former wife who had, since their divorce, been married to another man (Deut. 24:1-4).

Rabbinic resolution teaches that the circumstances as they seem to be reported in the Bible were misunderstood and thus the violations are denied (see ch. 26). All examples in this category have a similar type of resolution.

## 2. Violation Explained Away

This category differs from the preceding one in the following way: Whereas resolutions under the heading "Violation Denied" claim that once the

---

6. The work of Dr. David Berger, "On the Morality of the Patriarchs in Jewish Polemic and Exegesis Understanding Scripture," Paulist Press, pp. 49-62, was very helpful in this regard.

action or circumstances of the biblical character are clarified, the alleged violation falls away, resolutions under the heading "Violations Explained Away" claim that once the Torah law is clarified the alleged violation falls away. To be sure, this category also "denies" the violation: The distinction between these two categories can be seen clearly in the resolutions to Samson's violation of Nazirite law (Num. 6:6) by coming into contact with dead bodies (Judg. 14:19, 15:15). Two rabbinic passages offer the resolution that Samson either never touched his victims, or that he mortally wounded them and fled from the scene before they died. Thus, upon redefining the circumstances of Samson's actions we see that Samson did not violate the Torah in these instances, and for that reason these resolutions fall under the category, "Violation Denied."

Another rabbinic passage does not redefine Samson's action, but instead redefines the commandment of Samson's Naziriteship. This passage claims that the scope of the Torah's Nazirite law was never intended to apply to Samson. Thus the violation is explained away based on this understanding of Torah law (see ch. 12).

### 3. Temporary Measure (*Hora'at Sha'ah*)

A temporary measure (*hora'at sha'ah*) is the ultimate justification for apparent wrongdoing. This category differs from the preceding two in the following way. The resolutions listed under "Violations Denied" clarify a possible misunderstanding of the perpetrator's action. The resolutions listed under "Violations Explained Away" clarify a possible misunderstanding of the Torah commandment. The "Temporary Measure" category admits that the perpetrator's action as well as the Torah commandment have been properly understood. However, the violation of Torah law is warranted by the situation at hand.

The resolutions in this category are broken down into subdivisions:

1.  Apparent violations performed by a prophet or a leader,[7] which are warranted by the situation at hand. God does not seem to issue the command in these instances. The following case is a sample of the category. When the Ark of the covenant was returned to Israel from the Philistines, the people of Bet Shemesh presented cows as burnt offerings outside the Tent of Meeting (I Sam. 6:14). the text is silent regarding the violation of Torah law requiring that burnt offerings be male animals sacrificed at the Tent of Meeting (Lev. 1:3). Rabbinic resolution teaches that the men of Bet Shemesh acted under the rules of *hora'at sha'ah* (see ch. 16).

2.  A *hora'at sha'ah* by divine decree.[8] These include instances where God specifically orders someone to violate the law. A sample from this category is God's charge to Gideon to violate several Torah laws regarding sacrifice (Judg. 6:25-26) (see ch. 38).

Apparent violations belonging to the first subdivision are interspersed with the other resolutions. Apparent violations belonging to the second subdivision are included in a separate section at the end of the study. This is due to the fact that when God specifically orders someone to violate the law, surely the narrator cannot be expected to report it as a violation. Yet this subdivision is included in this study because the phenomenon recurs relatively often in the books of Joshua, Judges, and Samuel.

A sub-category of *hora'at sha'ah* absolves the king of an apparent violation of Torah law based on his special rights as ruler. This resolution is

---

7. *Hora'at sha'ah* means a "*ruling* under special dispensation" or an "emergency *ruling*." This term seems to indicate that the rule only applies to one who is capable of *hora'ah* or offering a binding decision. Thus we only find *hora'at sha'ah* relating to kings, prophets, judges or rabbis, in rabbinic literature.

8. See J. Babad, *Minhat Hinnukh*, vol. II, comm. 516. There, the opinion is expressed that *all* acts of *hora'at sha'ah* must be by the word of God. See, however, Tosafot, *Yevamot* 90b, s.v. *ve-ligmar*; Tosafot, *Sanhedrin* 89b, s.v. *Eliyahu*. This opinion maintains that a prophet, on his own initiative, can violate the Torah based on *hora'at sha'ah*.

narrowly defined in rabbinic literature as the right of the king to kill anyone who defies his command (*mored be-malkhut*) (see BT *Sanhedrin* 49a).

We find this only once in rabbinic literature regarding the violations listed in this study. David justifies his reason for wanting to kill Nabal because "Nabal rebelled against the king" (see ch. 24).[9]

In post-rabbinic literature, the special rights of a king are broadened. Rav maintains that these rights move beyond the privileges of the king: *kol ha-omer ba-parashat ha-melekh, melekh muttar bo* (BT *Sanhedrin* 20b). Rav is referring to the liberties of the king mentioned in I Sam. 8:11-20. However, this section deals with the right of the king to kill someone even if, according to Torah law, he does not deserve to die.

For instance, the king can kill a murderer who could not be convicted in a court of Jewish law (see ch. 28). This license was further broadened to include not only the right to kill someone who deserved the death penalty (but could not be convicted in a court of Jewish law), but to kill somebody who is not guilty of a capital crime. Thus, if a king feels the need to have someone killed in order to correct a situation, he can have that person killed (see ch. 20-21; 31; 34-35).

The special rights of a king also license him to rule leniently in certain cases. For instance, if the Torah demands the death penalty for a certain crime, the king can absolve the person of that penalty (see ch. 33 note 154).

Thus we see that although the rabbinic discussion of the special rights of the king regarding the taking of a subject's life is limited to the principle of *mored be-malkhut*, post-rabbinic authors expanded those rights. Commentators who played significant roles in the discussion of the special rights of the king include Rambam, Ralbag, Abravanel and Malbim.

---

9. The term *mored be-malkhut* is also found in rabbinic literature regarding Joab and Amasa (BT *Sanhedrin* 49a), Uriah the Hittite (BT *Shabbat* 56a) and Ahithophel (BT *Bava Batra* 147a). For a list of all biblical cases of *mored be-malkhut*, see *Otzar Yisrael* [Hebrew], ed. J.D. Eisenstein, New York, 1911, vol. 6, pp. 133b-134a.

## 4. Violation Acknowledged

This category consists of those instances in which the Rabbis acknowledge violations of Torah law, despite the fact that the biblical text seems to be unaware that a violation of Torah law has taken place. This is unusual, because the Rabbis often explain away apparent violations even when they are explicitly mentioned in the biblical text.

A sample of this category is the rabbinic acknowledgement that David, in seeking the welfare of the Ammonites (II Sam. 10:2), violated the Torah (Deut. 23:7) (see ch. 30). In such cases, the Rabbis will usually identify some type of punishment that results for this wrongdoing insofar as the text does not explicitly recognize the wrongdoing.

## 5. Violation Acknowledged and Excused

The first three categories of this study account for the biblical narrator's apparent unawareness of violation by postulating that, in effect, no violation has occurred. The fourth category acknowledges violation and often suggests that the biblical author really acknowledged the violation as well. The fifth category, "Violation Acknowledged and Excused," recognizes the violation but excuses it.

A sample of this category is the rabbinic source which excuses the Israelites for putting off the building of the Temple for so long. The Israelites, the source claims, had too many talebearers among them and this drove away God's presence (see ch. 6). The failure of the Israelites to build the Temple is excused; no punishment is mentioned.

## 6. Violation Ignored

This category includes all violations for which, after careful research, no discussion could be found in rabbinic literature.[10] For example, no rabbinic

---

10. In each instance, however, post-rabbinic sources are quoted, which considered these actions to be in apparent violation of Torah law. In some instances resolutions

resolution could be found which deals with David's violation of Torah law in possessing a graven image (I Sam. 19:13).[11]

---

are provided, and in others, the violation is acknowledged without resolution. Whether or not resolutions are provided seems to be based on the character of the perpetrator. If the teraphim were found in Nabal's house (Cf. I Sam. 25), there is no doubt that rabbinic or post-rabbinic literature would condemn him as an idolater. (The Rabbis condemn Nabal as such nonetheless; see *Midrash Tehillim* 53:1). However, no one condemns David for having teraphim in his house, and post-rabbinic sources abound, explaining the purpose the teraphim served.

11. See Radak, I Sam. 19:13, who quotes a midrashic source no longer extant. Even if we use the source the resolution is still quite unclear. Modern scholars explain the teraphim as aids to fertility, explaining Rachel's association with them (Gen. 31:34). Such an explanation is clearly foreign to the rabbinic approach to biblical characters considered righteous. Rachel knew teraphim were of no use. She hid them from her father to prevent him from using them to find where Jacob went. The *Ketav Sofer* (Rabbi Abraham Samuel Benjamin Sofer, 1815-1871) explains Rachel's action in this light. See also Ezek. 21:26 and Zech. 10:2.

# Chapter 1
# Violation Related to Idolatry

| Torah | |
|---|---|
| Exod. 20:3-5 | You shall have no other gods beside Me. You shall not make for yourself a sculptured image, or any likeness of what is in the heavens above, or on the earth below, or in the waters under the earth. You shall not bow to them or serve them. |

| Prophets | |
|---|---|
| Josh. 5:14 | He replied, "No, I am a captain of the Lord's host. Now I have come!" Joshua threw himself face down to the ground, and prostrating himself, said to him, "What does my lord command of his servant?" |

## Description of Violation

The commandments "You shall have no other gods beside me" and "You shall not bow down to them" ban every type of worship but that dedicated to God.[12] Why did Joshua bow down to the angel, and why wasn't he reprimanded for violating the law?

---

12. See *Mekhilta*, Yitro 6, BT *Rosh Hashanah* 24b, which includes angels in the prohibition of bowing to graven images. BT *Sanhedrin* 61b permits prostration before a human if not done as an act of worship (see Tosafot, ibid., s.v. *Rava*). See also *Torah Temimah*, Esth. 3:2 (ז), regarding why Mordecai refused to bow to Haman. The implication that emerges from this is that all acts of prostration before an angel are prohibited. See also Rambam, *Hilkhot Akum* 1:2, Ramban, Exod. 20:3, s.v. *E-lohim*, Joseph Albo, *Sefer ha-Ikkarim* 3:18.

| Rabbinic Resolution | |
|---|---|
| BT *Megillah* 3a[13] | ויהי בהיות יהושע ביריחו וישא עיניו וירא והנה איש עומד לנגדו וחרבו שלופה בידו. וילך יהושע אליו ויאמר לו, הלנו אתה אם לצרינו? ויאמר, לא כי אני שר צבא ה' עתה באתי. ויפל יהושע על פניו ארצה וישתחו (יהושע ה:יג-יד). והיכי עביד הכי? ... אסור לאדם שיתן שלום לחבירו בלילה חיישנן שמא שד הוא. שאני התם דאמר ליה כי אני שר צבא ה'...ודלמא משקרי? גמירי דלא מפקי שם שמים לבטלה. |
| | Once, when Joshua was near Jericho, he looked and saw a man standing before him, drawn sword in hand. Joshua went up to him and asked him, "Are you one of us or of our enemies?" He replied, "No, I am captain of the Lord's host. Now I have come!" Joshua threw himself face down to the ground and prostrated himself (Josh. 5:13-14). But how could he do so? ... One may not greet his fellow at night for fear that he may be a demon. It was different there because he said to him, "I am captain of the Lord's host." But perhaps he was lying? We take it for granted that they do not utter the name of God in vain. |

## Analysis of Rabbinic Resolution

The Talmud only addresses the rabbinic transgression of greeting a stranger at night, ignoring the transgression of Exod. 20:5. The plain meaning of the passage therefore seems to indicate that Joshua's bowing to the angel is not considered a violation of law at all.[14] Thus no violation is acknowledged.

13. Also found in BT *Sanhedrin* 44a.
14. Rashi, however, explains that the Talmud, in asking "But how could he do so?" includes the obvious transgression of the bowing itself (BT *Megillah* 3a, s.v.

The silence of the Rabbis is problematic in light of the fact that rabbinic sources understand Scripture as prohibiting bowing to an angel. While rabbinic sources are silent, post-rabbinic materials abound on the subject of reconciling the apparent contradiction between Joshua's actions and the prohibition of bowing to an angel.[15]

---

*ve-heikhi avid hakhi*; BT *Sanhedrin* 44a, s.v. *ve-heikhi avid*). Thus the Talmud asks, "How could Joshua bow to someone he could not even greet at night?" The Talmud answers: since the angel used God's name it must have truly been an angel of the Lord. Thus, once Joshua was sure he was bowing to a real messenger of God, his act is permitted. See also Rashbam, Gen. 18:1, Exod. 3:4, regarding human interaction with angels. See also Rambam, *Moreh Nevukhim* 1:49, that the angel represents God Himself. This is not the type of angel referred to in note 12 above.
15. See Rambam, comm. to *Sanhedrin* 10 Yesod 5, for a philosophical approach to this prohibition. See also Joseph Albo, *Sefer ha-Ikkarim* 2:28, and Abravanel, *Rosh Amanah* 12, and Abravanel, Ralbag, Josh. 5:14.

# Chapter 2
# Violations Relating to the Conquest of the Land

| Torah | |
|---|---|
| Deut. 7:1-2 | When the Lord your God brings you to the land that you are about to invade and occupy, and He dislodges many nations before you—the Hittites, Girgashites, Amorites, Canaanites, Perizzites, Hivites, and Jebusites, seven nations much larger than you. And the Lord your God delivers them to you and you defeat them, you must doom them to destruction: grant them no terms and give them no quarters. |
| Deut. 20:16-17 | In the towns of the latter peoples which the Lord your God is giving you as a heritage, you shall not let a soul remain alive. You must proscribe them. The Hittites and the Amorites, the Canaanites and the Perizzites, the Hivites, and the Jebusites,[16] as the Lord your God has commanded you. |

---

16. There is a discrepancy between the two verses in Deuteronomy. The first verse cited mentions seven nations, and the second verse mentions six. The Girgashites are omitted in the second verse. The following sources nonetheless include Girgashites in the command for destruction: *Sifrei Devarim* 20:17, *Tanhuma, Bo* 72, commentary of *Etz Yosef* ad loc, Rashi, Exod. 13:5, s.v. *el eretz ha-kenaʾani*; Deut. 20:17, s.v. *ka-asher tzivekha*; Rambam, *Hilkhot Melakhim* 5:3; Ramban, Exod. 13:11, *ve-hayah ki yeviʾakha*. The following sources exclude Girgashites from the command for destruction: JT *Sheviʾit* 6:1 (19a); Rashi, Exod. 33:2, s.v. *ve-gerashti et ha-kenaʾani*. Rashi seems to be of two opinions. See *Pnei Moshe*, JT *Sheviʾit* 6:1 (18a), s.v. *savar Rav Imi* for a possible conciliation between the two opinions mentioned here.

| Prophets | |
|---|---|
| Josh. 6:17 | **A. Rahab**<br><br>The city [Jericho] and everything in it are to be proscribed for the Lord. Only Rahab is to be spared, and all with her in the house, because she hid the messengers we sent. |
| Josh. 9:20 | **B. Gibeonites**<br><br>This is what we will do to them [Gibeonites]. We will spare their lives, so that there be no wrath against us because of the oath that we swore to them. |
| | **C. Nations not Dispossessed** |
| Josh. 15:63 | But the Judites could not dispossess the Jebusites, the inhabitants of Jerusalem; so the Judites dwell with the Jebusites in Jerusalem to this day. |
| Josh. 16:10 | They failed to dispossess the Canaanites who dwelt in Gezer; so the Canaanites remained in the midst of Ephraim, as is still the case. But they had to perform forced labor. |
| Josh. 17:12-13 | The Manassites could not dispossess [the inhabitants of] these towns, and the Canaanites stubbornly remained in this region. When the Israelites became stronger, they imposed tribute on the Canaanites: but they did not dispossess them. |
| Judg. 1:21 | The Benjaminites did not dispossess the Jebusite inhabitants of Jerusalem; so the Jebusites have dwelt with the Benjaminites in Jerusalem to this day. |

| | |
|---|---|
| **Judg. 1:27-28** | Manasseh did not dispossess [the inhabitants of] Beth-Shean and its dependencies, or Taanach and its dependencies, or the inhabitants of Dan and its dependencies, or the inhabitants of Ibleam and its dependencies, or the inhabitants of Megiddo and its dependencies. The Canaanites persisted in dwelling in this region. And when Israel gained the upper hand, they subjected the Canaanites to forced labor; but they did not dispossess them. |
| **Judg. 1:29** | Nor did Ephraim dispossess the Canaanites who inhabited Gezer; so the Canaanites dwelt in their midst at Gezer. |
| **Judg. 1:30** | Zebulun did not dispossess the inhabitants of Kitron or the inhabitants of Nahalol, so the Canaanites dwelt in their midst but they were subjected to forced labor. |
| **Judg. 1:31-32** | Asher did not dispossess the inhabitants of Acco or the inhabitants of Sidon, Ahlab, Achzib, Helbah, Aphik and Rehob. So the Asherites dwelt in the midst of the Canaanites, the inhabitants of the land, for they did not dispossess them. |
| **Judg. 1:33** | Naphtali did not dispossess the inhabitants of Beth-Shemesh or the inhabitants of Beth-Anath. But they settled in the midst of the Canaanite inhabitants of the land, and the inhabitants of Beth-Shemesh and Beth-Anath had to perform forced labor for them. |
| **Judg. 1:35** | The Amorites also persisted in dwelling in Har-Heres, in Aijalon, and in Shaalbim. But the hand of the house of Joseph bore heavily on them and they had to perform forced labor. |

| Judg. 19:11-12 | Since they were close to Jebus, and the day was very far spent, the attendant said to his master, "Let us turn aside to this town of Jebusites and spend the night in it." But his master said to him." We will not turn aside to a town of aliens who are not of Israel, but will continue to Gibeah." |
|---|---|
| I Kings 9:20-21 | All the people that were left of the Amorites, Hittites and Perizzites, who were not of Israelite stock—those of their descendants who remained in the land and whom the Israelites were not able to annihilate—of these Solomon made a slave force, as is still the case. |

## Description of Violation

The Torah clearly expresses the fate in store for the seven nations of Canaan. Listed are three groups of apparent violations of this Torah law. The allowance made by the Israelites regarding Rahab and the Gibeonites may seem acceptable from the perspective of the biblical narrative itself, but still required justifications by the Rabbis. The verses regarding not dispossessing the other nations attest to the fact that many cities in Israel were inhabited by members of the seven nations after the conquest, and that some of these people lived in Israel for hundreds of years after the conquest.[17]

---

17. In addition, there are biblical characters such as Ahimelech the Hittite (I Sam. 26:6); Uriah the Hittite (II Sam. 11:3), and Aravnah the Jebusite (II Sam 24:16). BT *Kiddushin* 76b asserts that Uriah was not of Hittite stock, but an Israelite who came from the land once owned by the Hittites. Although there is no such assertion regarding Ahimelech in rabbinic literature, the same can be assumed of him. BT *Avodah Zarah* 24b asserts that Aravnah converted to Judaism. There are other instances in which the lands of the seven nations are mentioned in the books of Joshua, Judges, Samuel, and Kings. These are not necessarily indications that the people inhabiting these lands were members of the seven nations of Canaan. II Sam. 24:7, for instance, mentions the Canaanites and Hivites to describe a certain part of the land of Israel, once inhabited by those people who, by then, were presumably extinct.

| Rabbinic Resolutions – Rahab | |
|---|---|
| *Sifrei Bemidbar* **10:29** | ומה, מי שהיתה מעם שנאמר בו (דב' כ:טז) לא תחיה כל נשמה, על שקרבה עצמה כך קירבה המקום, ישראל שעושים את התורה, על אחת כמה וכמה? <br><br> If, because someone from a nation of which it is said "you shall not let a soul remain alive" (Deut. 20:16) drew close to God, in like manner, God drew her close to Himself. How much more so if Israel keeps the Torah? |
| BT *Megillah* **14b** | רחב הזונה התגיירה ונישא יהושע <br><br> Rahab the harlot converted and Joshua married her. |
| *Pesikta de-Rav Kahana*, Piska 13 | אמר הקדוש ברוך הוא לישראל, אני אמרתי לכם (דב' כ:יז) כי החרם תחרימם החתי והאמורי וכו', ואתם לא עשיתם כן. אלא (יהושע ו:כב) ואת רחב הזונה וגו' החיה. הרי ירמיהו בא מבניה של רחב הזונה ועשה לכם דברים של שכים בעיניכם.[18] <br><br> The Lord said to Israel: I said to you, "You shall utterly destroy the Hittites, Amorites..." (Deut. 20:17), and you did not do so. Instead, "Rahab the harlot is to be spared" (Josh. 6:22). Behold, in consequence, from her descendants will yet come Jeremiah who will make for you thorns in your eyes with his words. |

---

18. Cf. Num. 33:55, where the phrase *le-sikkim be-eineikhem* refers to the consequence of allowing foreigners to live among Israelites. See also Rashi, Jeremiah 1:1.

## Analysis of Rabbinic Resolutions

*Sifrei* and *Megillah* 14b state that Rahab was accepted into the congregation of Israel not only by Joshua but by God Himself, thus denying the violation. *Pesikta* acknowledges that Josh. 6:17 is in violation of Deut. 20:17; no justification for the violation is provided by this passage. The prevailing rabbinic opinion, however, with regards to Rahab is that she converted to Judaism, and as such no longer came under the biblical ban of Deut. 7:1-2 and 20:16-17.[19]

| Rabbinic Resolutions – the Gibeonites | |
|---|---|
| JT *Kiddushin* 4:1 (37a)[20] | אמרו, יודעים אנו שאמר הקב"ה לישראל (דב' כ:יז) כי החרם תחרימם החתי והאמרי וגו'. (דב' ז:ב) לא תכרת להם ברית וגו'. אלא הרי אנו הולכין ומרמין בהם, והם כורתים אתנו ברית. מה נפשך יהרגו אותנו יעברו על השבועה. יקיימנו אותנו עוברים על הגזרה. בין כך ובין כך נענשים ואנו יורשים את הארץ לעצמינו. |
| | They [the Gibeonites] said: We know that God said to Israel, "you shall utterly destroy them, the Hittites and the Amorites..." (Deut. 20:17) and "Grant them no terms" (Deut. 7:2). Let us trick them, and they will contract an agreement with us. If they kill us, they have violated an oath. If they allow us to live, they would be violating the decree. Either way they will be punished, and we will inherit the land for ourselves.[21] |

19. Post-rabbinic resolutions abound, justifying the allowance for Rahab to remain alive. See *Sefer Mitzvot Gedolot*, neg. 112; Tosafot, *Megillah* 14b, s.v. *de-igayyarah*; *Sotah* 35b, s.v. *le-rabbot*; *Gittin* 46a, s.v. *kevan*; Radak, Josh. 6:25.

20. This passage is elaborated upon in *Bemidbar Rabbah* 8:4.

21. If Israel violates the oath by killing the Gibeonites, the latter will obviously not inherit the land. See *Korban ha-Edah*, JT *Kiddushin* 4:1 (37a), *ve-anu yorshim et ha-aretz*, that some texts read *ve-ein yorshin et ha-aretz* meaning either way the Israelites will not inherit the land. Thus, their main objective was the destruction of Israel, even if they had nothing to gain by it.

| BT *Gittin* 46a | מי חלה שבועה עילוייהו? כיון דאמרו להו (יהושע ט:ט) מארץ רחוקה באנו, ולא באו, לא חיילה שבועה עילוייהו כלל. והאי דלא קטלינהו משום קדושת השם. |
| --- | --- |
| | Did the oath become binding at all? Since they [the Gibeonites] said, "we are from a far country" (Josh. 9:9), whereas they had not come from one, the oath was never binding. And the reasons why the Israelites did not slay them was because this would have impaired the sanctity of God's name. |

## Analysis of Rabbinic Resolutions

JT *Kiddushin* 4:1 expresses the evil intentions of the Gibeonites. *Bemidbar Rabbah* elaborates on this passage and shows how detestable the Gibeonites were to the Israelites throughout history.[22] BT *Gittin* 46a indicates that the Israelites indeed should have killed the Gibeonites, but doing so would have profaned the name of God, for the Israelites had sworn not to kill them.[23] Thus, even though the Gibeonites fall under the biblical ban of Deut. 7:1-2 and 20:16-17, Israel is justified in not killing them, and the violation is denied.

---

22. See also BT *Yevamot* 79a, where the Gibeonites are characterized by cruelty. This passage relates the thoughts of the Gibeonites, that the Israelites will be punished by God if they keep the oath. However, according to *Bemidbar Rabbah* 8:4 when Joshua hesitated to defend the Gibeonites when they were attacked, God Himself told Joshua that he must honor his oath to the Gibeonites.

23. JT *Kiddushin* 4:1 (37a) and BT *Gittin* 46a seem to indicate that the Gibeonites would have been destroyed if not for the oath. See, however, note 26 below, where the idea is expressed that the Gibeonites had the opportunity to join the ranks of Israel as did any other nation (See Josh. 11:19).

| Rabbinic Resolutions – Not Dispossessing the Nations | |
|---|---|
| *Sifrei Devarim* 12:17 | ואת היבוסי יושבי ירושלים לא יכלו בני יהודה להורישם. יכולים היו אבל אינן רשאין.<br><br>The Judites could not dispossess the Jebusites, the inhabitants of Jerusalem. They could have but were not allowed to. |
| *Pirkei de-Rabbi Eliezer* 36 [24] | אמרו בני חת לאברהם, יודעים אנו שעתיד הקב"ה ליתן לזרעך את כל הארצות האלה. כרות עמנו ברית שאין זרעך יורש מעיר יבוסי. וכרת עמהם ברית ואחר כך קנה מהם מערת המכפלה. מה עשו אנשי יבוס? עשו צלמי נחשת וכתבו עליהם ברית השבועה והעמידו אותם ברחוב העיר. וכשבאו ישראל לארץ, רצו ליכנס לעיר ולא היו יכולים מפני הברית שנ' (יהושע טו:סג) ואת היבוסי יושבי ירושלים לא יכלו בני יהודה להורישם.<br><br>The sons of Het said to Abraham we know God is destined to give these lands to you and your descendants. Make a covenant with us that your descendants will not inherit the city of Jebusites. And Abraham made with them a covenant, and afterwards bought from them the cave of Machpelah. What did the Jebusites do? They made copper images and wrote the covenant on it and set it up in the main street of the city, and when the Israelites came to the land, they wanted to enter the city but could not because of the covenant, as it is written, "The Judites could not dispossess the Jebusites, the inhabitants of the Jerusalem" (Josh. 15:63). |

---

24. For parallel passages, see Y. Kiel, *Da'at Mikra*, Josh. 15:63, p. 147, n. 159.

## Rabbinic Analysis

These passages explain that the sons of Judah could have physically dispossessed the Jebusites, but were not allowed to do so because of an oath taken by Abraham not to conquer this land. These passages would seem to resolve the violation posed by Judg. 1:21 and Judg. 19:11-12 as well. Thus, the violation is acknowledged and excused.[25]

No other violations are acknowledged, and no rabbinic resolutions are provided for not dispossessing the other nations. It would appear that the Rabbis understood the plain sense of Scripture as indicating, in all these instances, that the Israelites were not able militarily to dispossess the enemy, and therefore were not in violation of Torah law.[26]

---

25. See passages cited in previous note, which explain how David ultimately conquered this land, in violation of Abraham's oath.

26. This is the clear implication of *Gittin* 46a and *Sifrei Devarim* 12:17. Only the Judites were able to dispossess those who were allowed to remain in their midst. The other tribes were not able to dispossess those who remained in their midst. See Ramban, Deut. 20:11. According to Ramban, if the seven nations accept the seven Noachide laws they may live in Israel as forced laborers. However, if they accept the entire Torah, they are allowed to fully join the ranks of Israel. Ramban derives this ruling from I Kings 9:20, which states that Amorites, Hittites, and Perizzites, who were not of Israelite stock, were employed by Solomon as laborers. Ramban argues that this designation implies that other Amorites, Hittites, and Perizzites may be of Israelite stock, i.e., those who accepted the Torah. Those who accepted the seven Noachide laws were employed as laborers by Solomon. This answer can justify all traces of Canaanites in Israel after the conquest as long as it is clear that they did not cause the hearts of Israelites to sway from God and the Torah. See also J. Elizur, *Da'at Mikra*, Josh. 15:63, p. 147; Judg. 1:27-36 pp. 18-24. For a full account of rabbinic and Medieval sources relating to the status of the seven Canaanite nations regarding the conquest, see S. Krasner, *Nahalat Shimon: Joshua* (N.Y. 1978), ch. 7, pp. 57-61.

# Chapter 3
# Violation of the Law Against Vicarious Punishment

| Torah | |
| --- | --- |
| **Deut. 24:16** | A person shall be put to death only for his own crime. |

| Prophets | |
| --- | --- |
| **Josh. 7:5-6, 11** | The men of Ai killed about thirty-six of them... Joshua thereupon rent his clothes... But the Lord answered Joshua.... Israel has sinned. |

### Description of Violation

The Torah prohibits vicarious punishment. We find, however, in Josh. 7:5-6, 11, that thirty-six people died in the war against Ai as a consequence of Achan's sins (see Josh. 22:20). Thus vicarious punishment seems to be tolerated.

### Rabbinic Resolutions

No rabbinic resolution could be found which addresses this specific problem.[27] However, by analogy, the following passage may serve as a resolution for this problem even though it doesn't directly address the problem.

---

27. The following Talmudic passage raises the specific problem of vicarious punishment in Joshua 7, but does not offer a solution. The death of Yair ben Manasseh as consequence of Achan's sins is also an instance of vicarious punishment.

BT *Sanhedrin* 44a reads: Joshua cast down the articles stolen by Achan, before the Lord, exclaiming, God, for these shall a number equal to the majority of the Sanhedrin be killed? For it is written, "and the men of Ai smote of them about thirty-six men" (Josh. 7:5), regarding which it was taught, literally thirty-six men; this is R. Judah's view. R. Nehemiah said to him: were there actually thirty-six? Surely only *about* thirty-six men is written. But this refers to Yair ben Manasseh who was equal in importance to the majority of the Sanhedrin.

| Midrash Tannaim, Deut. 24:16 | (דב' כד:טז) לֹא יומתו אבות על בנים. לפי שהוא אומר (שמ' כ:ה) פקד עון אבות על בנים, שומע אני אף מחוייבי בית דין. תלמוד לאמר לֹא יומתו אבות על בנים. |
|---|---|
| | "Parents shall not be put to death for children" (Deut. 24:16). Since Scripture states, "visiting the guilt of fathers upon their children" (Exod. 20:5), I might have thought that such is the case even pertaining to those guilty of capital crimes.[28] Therefore, Scripture states parents shall not be put to death for children. |

### Analysis of Rabbinic Resolution

This passage indicates that the courts have no right to punish one person for the sins of another. However, the heavenly court does punish one for the sins of another, as Exod. 20:5 indicates. The thirty-six people who died as a consequence of Achan's sins were not put to death by the earthly court. Thus no vicarious punishment is executed and the violation is explained away.[29]

---

28. That a child can be put to death by the courts for a capital crime committed by his father. This cannot be done. But God *can* visit the guilt of one party on another. See Talmudic resolutions to Exod. 20:5 and Deut. 24:16 at BT *Berakhot* 7a and BT *Makkot* 24a.

29. For a rabbinic discussion on the different applications of Exod. 20:5 and Deut. 24:16, see Manasseh ben Israel's *Conciliator*, vol. I, #104, pp. 164-167. Abravanel and Ralbag explain the problem of this discussion in the following way: the thirty-six men didn't die as a *direct* consequence of Achan's sins as the text may imply. Achan, by his sins, caused the withdrawal of God's providence from the whole community of Israel, whereupon it became vulnerable to the vicissitudes of life and death.

# Chapter 4
# Violation of Proper Judicial Procedure

| Torah | |
|---|---|
| **Deut. 17:6** | A person shall be put to death only on the testimony of two or more witnesses; he must not be put to death on the testimony of a single witness. |

| Prophets | |
|---|---|
| **Josh. 7:20-26** | Achan answered Joshua, "It is true, I have sinned against the God of Israel" ... then Joshua and all Israel with him, took Achan... and all Israel pelted him with stones. They raised a huge mound of stones over him which is still there. |

### Description of Violation

Torah law requires the testimony of two witnesses for conviction of a criminal offense. How then was Achan killed in the absence of testimony?

| Rabbinic Resolution | |
|---|---|
| BT *Sanhedrin* 43b [30] | הלך והפיל גורלות ונפל הגורל על עכן. אמר לו, "יהושע בגורל אתה בא אלי?" אמר לי, "בבקשה ממך אל תוציא לעז על הגורלות שעתיד ארץ ישראל שתתחלק בגורל... תן תודה.... |
| | He went and cast lots, and the lot fell upon Achan. He said to him, "Joshua, will you convict me with a mere lot [i.e., without the testimony of two witnesses]?" ... Joshua said to Achan, "Please do not slander lots, for Israel is yet to be divided by means of lots.... therefore admit your guilt." |

**Analysis of Rabbinic Resolution**

It would seem that no testimony at all was needed. God, in fact, ordered that the lots be cast (see Josh. 7:13-14), thus guaranteeing that the lot will fall on the guilty party. Joshua only asks for a confession so as not to slander the lots. Had it not been for this fear, Joshua would have had Achan put to death on the basis of the evidence from Heaven alone.[31] Thus, the violation is denied.

---

30. This passage can also be found in JT *Sanhedrin* 6:3 (20b); *Tanhuma*, Vayyeshev 2; *Pirkei de-Rabbi Eliezer* 38; *Eliyahu Rabbah* 18.

31. See Rambam, *Hilkhot Sanhedrin* 18:6, where it is suggested that Joshua's decision was a *hora'at sha'ah* or that it was based on his special legal right as king, to kill violators of his precepts or rulings. See Joshua 1:18, which is used by Rambam (*Hilkhot Melakhim* 3:8) to derive that Joshua did indeed have the rights of a king.

# Chapter 5
## Violation of Deut. 24:16

| Torah | |
|---|---|
| **Deut. 24:16** | Parents shall not be put to death for children, nor children be put to death for parents. |

| Prophets | |
|---|---|
| **Josh. 7:24-25** | Then Joshua took Achan, son of Zerah, and the silver, and the mantle, and the wedge of gold, his sons and his daughters, and his ox, his ass and his flock, and his tent, and all his belongings and all Israel with him, and they brought them up to the Valley of Achor. And all Israel pelted him with stones. They put them to the fire and stoned them. |

### Description of Violation

Torah law, it seems, does not allow children to suffer for the sin of their parents. How then, is Achan's guilt passed onto his children as well? This seems to be contrary to the spirit of this law.

| Rabbinic Resolution | |
|---|---|
| BT *Sanhedrin* 44a [32] | אם הוא חטא, בניו ובנותיו מה חטאו? אמר ליה, ולטעמיך אם הוא חטא כל ישראל מה חטאו? דכתיב "וכל ישראל עמו" (יהושע ז:כד) אלא לרדותן. הכי נמי כדי לרדותן. |
| | If he sinned, wherein did his sons and daughters sin? He retorted: on your view one might ask. If he sinned, how did all Israel sin that it is written, "And all Israel with him" (Josh. 7:24)[33]? But it was to overawe them.[34] So here, too it was to overawe them.[35] |
| *Pirkei de-Rabbi Eliezer* 38 | לקח יהושע את עכן ואת הכסף ואת האדרת ואת לשון הזהב ואת בניו ואת בנותיו ואת כל אשר לו והעלם בעמק עכור. (דב' כד:טז) לא יומתו אבות על בנים ובנים לא יומתו על אבות. אם כן אלו מפני מה מתו? אלא על שידעו בדבר ולא הגידו. |
| | Joshua took Achan, and the silver, the mantle and the wedge of gold, his sons and his daughters, and all his belongings and brought them up to the Valley of Achor. But it is written, "parents shall not be put to death for children, nor children be put to death for parents" (Deut. 24:16). If so, why were these killed? Because they knew of Achan's actions and did not tell. |

32. See also *Bemidbar Rabbah* 23:6; *Tanhuma*, Masei 5.
33. If one will ask how Achan's children can be punished for a crime they did not commit, one can also find reason to ask how all Israel were punished for a crime they did not commit, for the end of the verse suggests that "all Israel with them" shared Achan's fate.
34. All Israel were taken to the place of execution to be overwhelmed by his punishment.
35. Thus his family was not killed with him, but were brought there to witness the execution with all Israel.

## Analysis of Rabbinic Resolution

BT *Sanhedrin* 44a implies that Achan's children were not killed,[36] thus no violation occurred. *Pirket de-Rabbi Eliezer* 38 admits that Achan's children were killed.[37] It explains that they deserved to die for not disclosing Achan's sin,[38] thus the violation is denied.

---

36. See Rashi, Ralbag, Abravanel, Josh. 7:25, who explain that, as the verse states, all Israel stoned *him* (Achan) with stones, and burned *them* (tent and moveables) with fire, and stoned *them* (beasts) with stones. Therefore, the children were not put to death, and the teaching of the Torah law was not violated.

37. Thus, "They put them to the fire and stoned them" refers to Achan and his children.

38. For had they immediately revealed Achan's sin, the calamity of Ai could have been avoided, for God said, "You will not be able to stand up to your enemies until you have purged the proscribed from among you" (Josh. 7:13). Thus, according to *Pirkei de-Rabbi Eliezer* the burden of death of thirty-six men lay on the heads of Achan's children as well. Radak explains that the killing of Achan's children is indeed in violation of "nor shall children be put to death for parents" (Deut. 24:16). However, it is in agreement with the idea behind "visiting the guilt of the fathers upon the children" (Exod. 20:5). In respect to human judges, the license to take the life of children for sins of fathers is not accorded. However, within the supreme authority of God, the father's sins may be visited on the son. In the present case, Joshua slew the children of Achan by command of God (Josh. 7:15). Thus we can further explain, according to *Pirkei de-Rabbi Eliezer*, how Achan's children were killed for Achan's sins without Torah law being violated. See also BT *Shevuot* 39a, "If he sinned, did his family sin too?"

# Chapter 6
# Failure to Build a Temple to God
# at the Appointed Time

| Torah | |
|---|---|
| **Deut. 12:5** | Look only to the site that the Lord your God will choose amidst all your tribes to establish His name there. Seek for Him a habitation and go there. |
| **Deut. 12:10-11** | When you cross the Jordan and settle in the land that the Lord your God is allotting you, and He grants you safety from all your enemies around you, and you live in security, then you must bring everything that I command you to the site where the Lord your God will choose to establish His name. |

| Prophets | |
|---|---|
| **Josh. 23:1** | Much later after the Lord had given Israel rest from all their enemies around them, and when Joshua was old and well advanced in years.... |

### Description of Violation

The conditions necessary for the building of the Temple were met in Josh. 23:1. Nonetheless, the Temple was not built until the days of Solomon. Why did the Israelites wait so long to build the Temple?

| Rabbinic Resolutions | |
|---|---|
| *Devarim Rabbah* 5:10 | על שלשה דברים נצטוו ישראל בכניסתן לארץ. ואלו הן למחות זכרו של עמלק ולמנות להם מלך ולבנות להם בית הבחירה. ומנו להם מלך ומחו זכרו של עמלק. ולמה לא בנו להם בית המקדש? שהיו דילטורין ביניהם.<br><br>Three commandments were given to the Israelites when they entered the land: To wipe out the remnant of Amalek, to appoint a King, and to build a Temple.[39] They appointed a king and they wiped out the remnant of Amalek. If so, why did they not build the Temple [in the days of Saul]? Because there were talebearers among them. |
| *Midrash Tehillim* 17 | כל אותן אלפים שנפלו במלחמה בימי דוד, לא נפלו אלא על שלא תבעו בנין בית המקדש<br><br>Thousands of people died in wars in David's day because they did not demand the building of the Temple. |

## Analysis of Rabbinic Resolutions

*Devarim Rabbah* 5:10 indicates that Saul could not build the Temple because of the nature of the people in his time.[40] This is not a justification of the failure of the Israelites to build the Temple, but it excuses them nonetheless. Only a worthy Israelite community may undertake to build the Temple. Thus the violation is excused.[41]

---

39. This order does not conform to the order of the commandments in the Torah, nor does it conform to the order mentioned in BT *Sanhedrin* 20b. H. Zundel's *Etz Yosef* suggests that the order in *Devarim Rabbah* be emended to conform with the order in BT *Sanhedrin* 20b, which reads (1) to appoint a king (2) to wipe out the remnant of Amalek (3) to build the Temple.

40. BT *Sotah* 42a: "Four groups do not receive the Divine Presence: ... a group of talebearers." The talebearers in Saul's day drove away the Divine Presence.

41. This passage does not question why the Israelites failed to build the Temple before the days of Saul. It seems to follow the rabbinic teaching of BT *Sanhedrin* 20b, that the appointment of a king precedes the building of the Temple. Therefore,

When the conditions necessary for the building of the Temple were met in David's time, he asks to build the Temple.[42] David is turned down because he had shed much blood (I Chron. 22:8-9). Nonetheless, *Midrash Tehillim* 17 indicates that the Israelites of David's time were punished for not building the Temple. Only David was excused from performing this commandment. This did not excuse the nation from taking the initiative.[43] Thus the violation is acknowledged, and the people were punished for the violation.

---

prior to Saul's day, failure to build the Temple was not viewed by the Rabbis as a violation. According to *Shemot Rabbah* 48:4, Moses was also considered a king. Rambam, *Hilkhot Melakhim* 3:8, maintains that Joshua was also considered a king. Abravanel, in his introduction to Judges, says the same regarding all the leaders of Israel between Joshua and Saul. The Talmud, however, considers Saul to be the first king of Israel insofar as his position, to the exclusion of leaders before him, necessitated the destruction of Amalek and the building of the Temple. Perhaps even according to the views cited above, failure on the part of leaders before Saul to destroy Amalek and to build the Temple was not viewed as a violation.

42. The conditions are seen in II Sam. 7:1: "When the king was settled in his place and the lord had granted him safety from all the enemies around him."

43. So Radak, II Sam. 24:25. See however, Rambam, *Moreh Nevukhim* 3:45, for the role of the king in the building of the Temple. See also R. Marguiles, *Margaliyyot ha-Yam* (Jerusalem, 1958), p. 96.

# Chapter 7
## Failure to Appoint a King

| Torah | |
|---|---|
| Deut. 17:14-15 | If, after you have entered the land that the Lord your God has given you, and occupied it and settled in it, you decide, "I will set a king over me, as do all the nations about me," you shall set a king over yourself.... |

| Prophets | |
|---|---|
| Josh. 23:1 | Much later after the Lord had given Israel rest from all their enemies around them, and when Joshua was old and well advanced in years.... |

### Description of Violation

In the days of Joshua, Israel entered the land of Israel, they occupied it, settled in it, and rested from their enemies around them. Thus the conditions necessary for the appointment of a king were met. Why, then, did the Israelites not appoint a king at the time?

| Rabbinic Resolution | |
|---|---|
| BT *Sanhedrin* 20b | לא נאמרה פרשה זו אלא כנגד תרעומתן שנאמר, (דב' יז:טו) ואמרת אשימה עלי מלך<br><br>This chapter was written in anticipation of their future murmurings, as it is written, "And shall say I will appoint a king over me" (Deut. 17:15). |

## Analysis of Rabbinic Resolution

This passage indicates that the Torah only meant to *permit* the Israelites to have a king, not to command them to do so. The Torah allows the Israelites to appoint a king if they feel the need for one.[44] Such a need was not felt until the days of Gideon[45] and the days of Samuel.[46] Thus there was no violation in not appointing a king earlier.[47]

---

44. Deut. 17:15: "If... you decide, I will set a king over me.... You will set a king over yourself." According to our source, until this desire surfaces it is not obligatory to appoint a king. See Ibn Ezra, R. Bahya, Abravanel, S.D. Luzzatto, Deut.17:15.
45. See below ch. 9.
46. See below ch. 17.
47. See also *Midrash Ha-Gadol*, Balak 24:19, which seems to address the issue of why the Israelites first asked for a king in Samuel's day.

# Chapter 8
# Violations Regarding Sacrifice

| Torah | |
|---|---|
| **Lev. 17:8-9** | If any man... offers a burnt offering as a sacrifice, and does not bring it to the entrance of the Tent of Meeting to offer it to the Lord, that man shall be cut off from his people. |
| **Deut. 12:13-14** | Take care not to sacrifice your burnt offerings any place you like, but only in the place which the Lord will choose in one of your tribal territories. |

| Prophets[48] | |
|---|---|
| **1. Judg. 2:4-5** | As the angel of the Lord spoke these words to the Israelites, the people broke into weeping. So they named that place Bochim, and they offered sacrifices to the Lord. |
| **2. Ibid. 13:19** [49] | Manoah took the kid and the meal offering and offered them up on the rock to the Lord. |

---

48. This list, beginning from the book of Judges, is incredible in the backdrop of the fact that the Israelites had almost been driven to war over this issue at Joshua chapter 22.

49. This list omits one of the most extensive single lists of apparent sacrificial violations in the entire Bible. BT *Temurah* 28b lists no less than eight violations committed by Gideon at Judg. 6:25-26, against normal sacrificial procedure. And while both Gideon and Manoah, in this case of Judg. 13:19, are considered to have acted under guidelines of *hora'at sha'ah*, since Gideon acted under the explicit direction of God, his sacrifice is not included. Surely someone acting under God's direction cannot be considered to be in violation or ignorant of the Torah. See below, ch. 38.

| | |
|---|---|
| **3. Ibid. 20:26** | Then all the Israelites, all the army, went up and came to Bethel and they sat there, weeping before the Lord. They fasted that day until evening, and presented burnt offerings and offerings of well-being to the Lord. |
| **4. Ibid. 21:2-4** | The people came to Bethel and sat there before God until evening.... Early the next day, the people built an altar then, and they brought burnt offerings and offerings of well-being. |
| **5. I Sam. 6:15** | Then the men of Beth-Shemesh presented burnt offerings and other sacrifices to the Lord that day. |
| **6. Ibid. 7:7-9** | The Israelites had assembled at Mizpah... and they implored Samuel, "Do not neglect us...." Thereupon Samuel took a suckling lamb and sacrificed it as a whole burnt offering to the Lord. |
| **7. Ibid. 7:17** | Then he [Samuel] would return to the Ramah, for his home was there, and there too he would judge Israel. He built an altar there to the Lord. |
| **8. Ibid. 9:12** | "...the people have a sacrifice at the shrine today. As soon as you enter the town [Zuph] you will find him...." |
| **9. Ibid. 11:15** | All the people went to Gilgal, and there at Gilgal they declared Saul king before the Lord. They offered sacrifices of well-being there before the Lord. |
| **10. Ibid. 13:8-9** | ... When Samuel failed to come to Gilgal, and the people began to scatter, Saul said, "Bring me the burnt offering and the sacrifice of well being." |
| **11. Ibid. 16:4-5** | When he came to Bethlehem... he replied, "I have come to sacrifice to the Lord. Purify yourselves and join me in the sacrificial feast." |
| **12. Ibid. 20:6** | If your father notes my absence, you say, "David asked my permission to run down to his home town, Bethlehem, for the whole family has its annual sacrifice there." |

| 13. II Sam. 6:13 | When the bearers of the Ark of the Lord had moved six paces, he sacrificed an ox and fatling. |
|---|---|
| 14. Ibid. 6:17 | They brought in the Ark of the Lord and set it up in its place inside the tent which David had pitched for it, and David sacrificed burnt offerings and offerings of well-being before the Lord. |
| 15. Ibid. 15:12 | Absalom also sent to fetch Ahithophel the Gilonite, David's counselor, from his town, Giloh, when the sacrifices were to be offered. |
| 16. Ibid. 24:25 | And David built there an altar to the Lord and sacrificed burnt offerings and offerings of well being. |
| 17. I Kings 3:4 [50] | The king went to Gibeon to sacrifice there, for that was the largest shrine; on that altar Solomon presented a thousand burnt offerings. |
| 18. Ibid. 18:20-24 | Ahab sent orders to all the Israelites and gathered the prophets at Mount Carmel. Then Elijah said to the people, ... "Let two young bulls be given to us. Let them choose one bull, cut it up, and lay it on the wood, but let them not apply the fire; I will prepare the other bull, and lay it on the wood, and will not apply fire. You will then invoke your god by name, And I will invoke the Lord by name; and it shall be, the god who responds with fire, that one is God." |

---

50. The verse just before this one, I Kings 3:3, indicates that sacrifice at shrines was looked down upon, even prior to the building of the Temple. The verse reads, "And Solomon, though he loved the Lord and followed the practices of his father, David, also sacrificed and offered at shrines." See Radak and Abravanel, I Kings 3:4, who explain that even during the time of *hetter bamot* (see resolutions below) it was still preferable to offer sacrifices at the Tent of Meeting. The corresponding verse to I Kings 3:4 in II Chron. 1:3 stresses the fact that the Tent of Meeting was at Gibeon when Solomon sacrificed there.

## Description of Violation

The Torah restricts the offering of sacrifice, to the Tent of Meeting or the place of God's choice. Yet there are many verses which attest to the fact that sacrifices were offered outside the Tent of Meeting, and such seems to be tolerated by the text.

| Rabbinic Resolution | |
| --- | --- |
| **BT *Zevahim* 112b** | עד שלא הוקם המשכן היו הבמות מותרות ועבודה בבכורות, ומשהוקם המשכן נאסרו הבמות ועבודה בכהנים.... באו לגלגל הותרו הבמות. באו לשילה נאסרו הבמות. באו לירושלים נאסרו הבמות ולא היה להן עוד היתר. <br><br> Before the Tabernacle was set up, shrines were permitted and the service was performed by the first born; after the Tabernacle was set up, shrines were forbidden and the service was performed by priests. When they came to Gilgal, shrines were again permitted. When they came to Shiloh, shrines were forbidden. When they came to Nob and to Gibeon, shrines were again permitted. When they came to Jerusalem, shrines were forbidden and were never again permitted. |
| **BT *Zevahim* 118b** | ימי אהל מועד שבמדבר ארבעים שנה חסר אחת. ימי אהל מועד שבגלגל ארבע עשרה. ימי אהל מועד שבנב וגבעון חמשים ושבע. נשתיירו לשילה ג' מאות ושבעים חסר אחת. <br><br> The duration of the Tent of Meeting in the wilderness was thirty-nine years, the duration of the Tent of Meeting at Gilgal was fourteen years.... The duration at Nob and Gibeon combined was fifty-seven years. The duration for Shiloh was three hundred sixty-nine years.[51] |

---

51. The sanctuary in the wilderness was built in the second year after the redemption from Egypt (Exod. 40:17), and the Temple was built 480 years after

## Analysis of Rabbinic Resolution

BT *Zevahim* 112b explains that at certain times, it was permitted to offer sacrifices outside the precincts of the Tent of Meeting. It was forbidden to do so when the Tent of Meeting stood at Shiloh and once the Temple was built in Jerusalem. Most of the verses cited occurred in times when shrines were permitted outside the precincts of the Tent of Meeting. Thus the violations in these verses are explained away. However, Judg. 2:4-5, 13:19, 20:26, 21:2-4, and 1 Kings 18:20-24 occurred in times when sacrifices outside the Tent of Meeting was forbidden. Upon closer scrutiny, Judg. 2:4-5 can be placed in the time when the Tent of Meeting was still at Gilgal, for even though this verse is in Judges, Joshua appears in the very next verse, thus indicating that this event occurred within the fourteen years that the Tent of Meeting stood at Gilgal.[52] Judg. 13:19 is addressed by the Rabbis in the following passage, and is permitted as an act of *hora'at sha'ah*.

| BT *Zevahim* 119b (#1) | מאי "ויקח מנוח..." (שופטים יג:יט) הוראת שעה היתה. |
| --- | --- |
| | How can we explain, "Manoah... offered it upon rock unto the Lord"[53]? It was a temporary measure. |

---

the redemption (I Kings 6:1). Thus the various sanctuaries stood for a total of 479 years. The amount of time that each sanctuary stood is derived by the Rabbis in BT *Zevahim* 118b-119a.

52. *Seder Olam Rabbah* 11. The tent of meeting was constructed at Shiloh toward the end of Joshua's lifetime. Joshua was alive at Judg. 2:6, thus leading to the assumption that Judg. 2:5 took place when the Tent of Meeting stood at Gilgal. Thus shrines were permitted and there was no violation.

53. At a time when such was forbidden, when the sanctuary stood at Shiloh.

| | |
|---|---|
| **BT *Zevahim* 119b (#2)** | כי לא באתם אל המנוחה ואל הנחלה (דב' יב:ז) מנוחה זו שילה נחלה זו ירושלים דברי רבי יהודה. רבי שמעון אומר מנוחה זו ירושלים נחלה זו שילה. תנא דבי ישמעאל זו וזו שילה. רבי שמעון בר יוחי אומר זו וזו ירושלים. |
| | "For you have not yet come to the rest and to the inheritance" (Deut. 12:7) — "rest" alludes to Shiloh, "inheritance" to Jerusalem; this is R. Judah's opinion. R. Simeon said: "Rest" alludes to Jerusalem, "inheritance" to Shiloh. The school of R. Ishmael taught: Both words allude to Shiloh. *R. Simeon bar Yohai said: Both words allude to Jerusalem.* |

The violations in Judg. 20:26 and 21:2-4 are not directly addressed in rabbinic literature. These verses are found in a chapter filled with stories of misguided people.[54] Perhaps for this reason, it was not necessary for the text or the Rabbis to address it. However, Rabbi Simeon bar Yohai, *Zevahim* 119b (#2), indirectly resolves not only the problems posed by Judg. 20:26 and 21:2-4, but the problems of Judg. 13:19 as well.

The view of R. Simeon bar Yohai is explained in the Talmud as follows: Since both "rest" (*menuhah*) and "inheritance" (*nahalah*) refer to the Temple in Jerusalem, there was no sanctuary before the Temple which put a "rest" to improvised altars outside the Tent of Meeting. Thus all shrines were permitted prior to the building of the Temple according to this opinion, and the violations are all explained away.

---

54. See below, chapter 14.

| Rabbinic Responses – I Kings 18:20-24 | |
|---|---|
| JT *Ta'anit* 2:8 (8b) | ויגש אליהו וגו' (מ"א יח:לו) ואליהו מקריב בחוץ בשעת איסור הבמות! אמר רבי שמלאי הקב"ה אמר לו שנאמר ובדבריך עשיתי (שם)<br><br>"Elijah came forward" (I Kings 18:36) — Elijah sacrificed outside the Temple at a time when it was forbidden! R. Simlai said. God told him to do so, as it says, I have done these things at your bidding (ibid.). |
| *Bereshit Rabbah* 85:5 | ויאמר לו אל-הים אני א-ל ש-די פרה ורבה גוי וקהל עמים יהיה ממך (בר' לה:יא) עתידין בניך לעשות כגוי וקהל עמים. מה קהל עמים מקריבין בשעת איסור במות, אף בניך מקריבין בשעת איסור במות.<br><br>"And God said to him, I am El Shad-dai. Be fertile and increase, an assembly of nations shall descend from you" (Gen. 35:11) — Your children are destined to act like the nations: just like the nations offer sacrifices of a forbidden nature at shrines, so your children will one day do so.[55] |
| BT *Yevamot* 90b | אליו תשמעון (דב' יח:טו) אפילו אומר לך עבור על אחת מכל מצות שבתורה כגון אליהו בהר הכרמל הכל לפי שעה, שמע לו.<br><br>"Unto him shall you listen" (Deut. 18:15) — even if he tells you to transgress any of the commandments of the Torah, as in the case, for instance, of Elijah on Mount Carmel, obey him in every respect in accordance with the needs of the hour. |

55. This refers to Elijah and the Israelites at Mt. Carmel. It cannot be claimed that the Midrash explains the verse as foreshadowing the Israelites' violation by means of offering sacrifices at forbidden shrines, a violation well documented in the book of Kings. According to the Midrash, the purpose of this verse is to inform Jacob of the good deeds his descendants will perform. Thus the passage was understood to refer to Elijah. See Tosafot, *Sanhedrin* 89b, s.v. *Eliyahu* (end).

| BT *Sanhedrin* 89b | המוותר על דברי נביא. מנא ידע דאיעניש? דיהיב ליה אות. והא מיכה דלא יהיה ליה אות ואיעניש! היכא דמוחזק שאני דאי לא תימא הכי.... אליהו בהר הכרמל הכי סמכי עליה ועבדי שחוטי חוץ? אלא היכא דמחזיק שאני. |
|---|---|
| | He who disregards the words of a prophet. But how does he know that he is a true prophet that he should be punished? If he gives him a sign. But Micah did not give a sign yet he was punished! (I Kings 20:35-36). If he was well established as a prophet it is different. For if you would not consider this... how could the people listen to Elijah at Mount Carmel and sacrifice outside the Temple? Hence the case, where the prophet is well established, is different. |

All of these sources indicate that Elijah acted under the directive of God. Thus the violation is denied and is considered *hora'at sha'ah*.[56]

56. See Rambam, Introduction to *Perush Mishnayyot*, Mosad HaRav Kook edition (Jerusalem, 1961), p. 25, *Yesodei ha-Torah* 9:3, *Lehem Mishneh* ad loc. On the question of whether a prophet can only act as Elijah under the guidance of God, or even on his own accord, see the sources cited by *Encyclopedia Talmudit*, "hora'at sha'ah," vol. 8, p. 513, and cf. B. Oppenheimer, *Le-She'elat Rikkuz ha-Pulhan be-Yisrael* [Heb.], *Tarbiz* 28 (1959), pp. 138-153.

# Chapter 9

# Ignorance of a Command to Appoint a King

| Torah | |
|---|---|
| **Deut. 17:14-15** | If after you have entered the land that the Lord your God had given you, and occupied it and settled in it, you decide, "I will set a king over me, as do all the nations about me." You will set a king over yourself. |

| Prophets | |
|---|---|
| **Judg. 8:22-23** | Then the men of Israel said to Gideon, "Rule over us, you, your son and your grandson as well; for you have saved us from the Midianites." But Gideon replied, "I will not rule over you myself, nor shall my son rule over you; the Lord alone shall rule over you." |

### Description of Violation

If the Torah commands the appointment of a king, why did Gideon refuse the Israelites' request that he be their king? And why didn't the Israelites insist that they wanted to fulfill the precept?

## Rabbinic Resolution

This apparent violation is not addressed directly in rabbinic literature.[57] However in light of the discussion in Chapter 7, it would appear that Gideon successfully convinced the Israelites that their need for a king was not genuine.[58] Thus, Gideon's refusal to be king is not seen as a violation.[59]

---

57. Rabbinic literature regarding the appointment of a king addresses the Israelites' request for a king in the days of Samuel. This is because Samuel failed to convince his contemporaries that their need for a king was not genuine. Compare Judg. 8:22-23 and I Sam. 8:4-6.

58. See Meiri, *Horayot* 11b; Ibn Ezra, R. Bahya, S.D. Luzzatto, Deut. 17:15. These sources state that if the Israelites do not need a king, it is not obligatory to appoint one.

59. It is a curious fact that Gideon so calmly turned down the same request that so angered Samuel. See Ramban, Gen. 49:10; *Derashot ha-Ran* 11; Maharsha, *Sanhedrin* 20b, s.v. *ve-khein* (end).

# Chapter 10
# Violation of the Law of Murder

| Torah | |
|---|---|
| **Exod. 20:13** | You shall not murder. |

| Prophets | |
|---|---|
| **Judg. 11:30-32, 34, 39** | And Jephthah made the following vow to the Lord: "If you deliver the Ammonites into my hands, then whatever comes out of the door of my house to meet me on my safe return from the Ammonites shall be the Lord's and shall be offered by me as a burnt offering." Jephthah crossed over to the Ammonites and attacked them, and the Lord delivered them into his hands. When Jephthah arrived at his home in Mizpah there was his daughter coming to meet him... and he did to her as he had vowed. |

### Description of Violation

In light of the Torah's prohibition of murder,[60] why does the biblical text seem to approve of the ritual murder of Jephthah's daughter?

---

60. See the midrashic dialogue between Jephthah and his daughter (*Tanhuma*, Behukkotai 5).

| | **Rabbinic Resolution** |
|---|---|
| *Vayyikra Rabbah* 37:4 [61] | וידר יפתח נדר.... והיה היוצא וגו' (שופ' יא:ל-לא) אמר לו הקב"ה, אילו היה יוצא גמל או חמור או כלב הייתה מעלה אותו עולה לפני? מה עשה לו הקב"ה? השיבו שלא כהוגן, זימן לו את בתו, שנאמר, ויבא יפתח המצפה אל ביתו והנה בתו יוצאת לקראתו וגו' והיה כראותו אותה וגו' (שם:לד-לה). ולא היה יכול להתיר את נדרו? אלא אמר יפתח אני מלך איני הולך אצל פינחס. ופינחס אמר אני כהן גדול, איני הולך אצל עם הארץ. מבין דין לדין טפת ההיא עליבתא. ונתחייבו שניהם בדמיה.... יפתח היה נישול איברים ונקבר במקומות הרבה. ההא דכתיב, וימת יפתח ויקבר בערי גלעד (שופ' יב:ז) בעיר גלעד אין כתיב כאן אלא בערי גלעד, מלמד שהיה איבר נישול ממנו כאן ונקבר במקומו ואיבר נישול ממנו במקום אחר ונקבר במקומו. |
| | "And Jephthah made the following vow... then whatever comes out..." (Judg. 11:3-31) — God said to him, if a camel or a donkey or a dog had come out, would you have offered it as a burnt offering? So God answered him correspondingly by bringing him his daughter to hand, as it is written, "When Jephthah arrived at his home in Mizpah, his daughter was coming out to meet him. On seeing her, he rent his clothes" (Ibid. 34-35). But surely he could have had his vow disallowed [by going to Pinehas]. He said, "I am king, I will not go to Pinehas." Pinehas said, "I am High Priest, I will not go to an ignoramus." Between the two of them the poor maiden perished and both of them incurred responsibility for her death.... As regards Jephthah, limb after limb fell of his body and he was buried separately, as is proved by the text, "and he was buried in the cities of Gilead." This teaches that limb after limb after limb fell off his body and he was buried in many places. |

61. This passage can also be found in *Bereshit Rabbah* 60:3, *Tanhuma*, Behukkotai 5, and *Bereshit Rabbati*, p. 138. See also Eli Yassif's *Sippur Ben Sira Biymei ha-Benayim* (Jerusalem, 1984), p. 152 and 265, note 1.

## Analysis of the Rabbinic Resolution

This passage states that Jephthah sinned in fulfilling his vow, and that the biblical text itself indicates that Jephthah was punished for it.[62] Thus the violation is acknowledged.

---

62. Notwithstanding the fact that rabbinic sources understand that Jephthah killed his daughter, some Medieval sources suggest that Jephthah did not kill his daughter but that he sent her away to live the rest of her life in solitude. See Abravanel, Judg. 11:29-40, Radak and Malbim, Judg. 11:39. A reconciliation of these two opinions is offered by Ralbag, Judg. 11:39. See also Ramban's citation of Ibn Ezra, at Lev. 27:29, and Maharsha, *Taanit* 4a, s.v. *yakhol*. Regarding the burial of Jephthah in the "cities of Gilead," see Radak and Ralbag, Judg. 12:7. It is possible that the final words of Jephthah's vow, *ve-hayah la-YHVH ve-haʾalitihu olah*, "It will be unto God <u>and</u> I will offer it as a burnt offering," should be translated as, "It will be unto God [if a human] *or* as a burnt offering [in an animal]." This seems to be the plain meaning of BT *Taʾanit* 4a, and the Midrash cited above that suggest the worst case scenario of Jephthah's vow would be if an unclean animal emerged first from his house. Surely a much worse case *did* occur.

Ramban objects to this rendition because it implies that holiness comes to us only in seclusion, which is not a Jewish concept. Samuel was also dedicated to God (I Sam. 1:11), yet he did not live in seclusion. In fairness to Ibn Ezra, it is not the Tanakh rendering such a misconception of holiness, but Jephthah. Surely it would be preferable to consider Jephthah's mistaken understanding of holiness than to consider that he killed his daughter.

# Chapter 11
## Implied Violation of Kashrut Laws

| Torah | |
|---|---|
| Lev. 11:8 | You shall not eat of their flesh or touch their carcasses; they are unclean to you. |

| Prophets | |
|---|---|
| Judg. 13:4 | An angel of the Lord appeared to the woman and said to her... now be careful not to drink wine or other intoxicant, or eat anything unclean. |

### Description of Violation

The angel, in telling Samson's mother to avoid unclean foods, implies that prior to this declaration she normally ate unclean foods, or that such was permitted for all other Israelites. This would appear to contradict Lev. 11:8.

| Rabbinic Resolutions ||
|---|---|
| **BT *Sotah* 9b** | ועתה השמרי נא ואל תשתי יין ושכר ואל תאכלי כל טמא (שופ' יג:ד) מאי כל טמא? ותו עד השתא דברים טמאים קאכלה? ... דברים האסורים בנזיר.<br><br>Now be careful not to drink wine or other intoxicant or to eat anything unclean. What does "anything unclean" mean? Furthermore, had Samson's mother up to then eaten unclean things? ... She had up to then eaten things forbidden to a Nazirite. |
| ***Bemidbar Rabbah* 10:5** | ואל תאכלי כל טמא (שופ' יג:ד) ואין טמא אלא איסור שהתורה הזהירה לנזיר שלא לאכול כלום מכל אשר יוצא מגפן היין.<br><br>"Do not eat anything unclean" (Judg. 13:4), and "unclean" describes forbidden foods that the Torah warns a Nazirite not to eat from, mainly anything that comes from the grapevine. |

## Analysis of Rabbinic Resolution

These sources indicate that the unclean foods that Samson's mother was warned to refrain from were not ordinary unclean foods, but the foods that a Nazirite must refrain from, i.e., anything that comes from the grapevine.[63] She was accustomed to eating such foods, and all Israelites are of course permitted to eat such foods. Thus, the problem is solved, and the implied violation is denied.

---

63. Num. 6:3-4. See Radak, Judg. 13:4, Ralbag, Judg. 13:3.

# Chapter 12
## Violation of Nazirite Laws

| Torah | |
|---|---|
| **Num. 6:8-10** | Throughout the term that he has set apart for the Lord, he shall not go in where there is a dead person.... If a person dies suddenly near him... he shall shave his head... on the seventh day. On the eighth day he shall bring two turtledoves or two pigeons to the priest. |

| Prophets | |
|---|---|
| **Judg. 14:19** | He went down to Ashkelon and killed thirty of its men. He stripped them and gave the sets of clothing to those who had answered the riddle. |
| **Judg. 15:15** | He found a fresh jawbone of an ass and he picked it up, and with it killed a thousand men. |

### Description of Violation

Torah law forbids a Nazirite to come into contact with a dead body. How then did Samson kill people in these two instances? Also why didn't Samson subsequently perform the ritual described concerning a Nazirite who contacted defilement from a dead body? The biblical text seems to be unaware of these problems.

| Rabbinic Resolutions | |
|---|---|
| BT *Nazir* 4b (#1) | דלמי גרדויי גריד להו.<br><br>Perhaps he thrust it [the jawbone] at them without touching them. |
| BT *Nazir* 4b (#2) | דלמא גוססין שווין<br><br>Perhaps he mortally wounded them and they subsequently died.[64] |
| BT *Nazir* 4b (#3) | נזיר שמשון מותר ליטמא למתים שכן מצינו בשמשון שנטמא<br><br>A Nazir such as Samson is permitted to defile himself deliberately by contact with the dead, for Samson himself did so. |
| BT *Nazir* 4a (#4) | נזיר שמשון... אינו מביא קרבן טומאה<br><br>A Nazir such as Samson does not offer the sacrifice prescribed for defilement. |

*Nazir* 4b (#1) explains how Samson could have killed the Philistines without actually touching them. This passage only relates to Judg. 15:15, for according to Judg. 14:19, Samson took the clothes from his victims, thus obviously touching them. (#2) relates to both Judg. 14:19 and 15:15. Samson mortally wounded his victims and fled from the scene before they actually died. In this way, no defilement was contracted and Samson did not need to perform the subsequent ritual. Thus, the violation is denied.

(#3) and (#4), however, state that Samson did indeed touch his victims in both instances, but that he was never really considered a complete Nazir in the Torah sense. The only Nazirite laws pertaining to Samson were those enumerated in Judg. 13. Since no mention is made of defilement of the dead, Samson was permitted to come into contact with a dead body, and of course, no ritual was necessary subsequent to the deed.[65]

64. See *Nazir* 4b, Tosafot, s.v. *dilma*; Z.H. Chajes, ibid., s.v. *ve-dilma gosesin shavinhu*.
65. See Chapter 40. Also, BT *Nazir* 66a calls Samuel a Nazir like Samson, yet never questions his killing of Agag in I Sam. 15:33. See D. Cohen, *Ohel David* [Hebrew], (New York: 1979), vol. 2, pp. 23-25.

# Chapter 13

# Violation Concerning the Act of Suicide

| Torah | |
|---|---|
| **Gen. 9:5** | But for your own life-blood I will require a reckoning. I will require it of every beast; of men too will I require a reckoning for human life, of every man for that of his fellow men. |

| Prophets | |
|---|---|
| **Judg. 16:30** | Samson cried, "Let me die with the Philistines." And he pulled with all his might.... |
| **I Sam. 31:4-5** [66] | Saul said to his arms-bearer, "Draw your sword and run me through, so that the uncircumcised may not run me through and make sport of me." But his arms-bearer, in his great awe, refused; whereupon Saul grasped the sword and fell upon it. When his arms-bearer saw that Saul was dead, he too fell on his sword and died with him. |
| **II Sam. 17:23** | When Ahithophel saw that his advice had not been followed, he saddled his ass and went home to his native town. He set his affairs in order and then he hanged himself. |

66. Saul's request of the Amalekite lad to kill him in II Sam 1:8 is not treated here, for Saul would surely have died from the wounds he suffered in I Sam. 31:4-5. For this reason, Abimelech's request of his lad to kill him is not treated here, for he was also mortally wounded prior to the request. Zimri is also excluded from this list because of the unclear pronouns at I Kings 16:18.

## Description of Violations

The Torah prohibits the taking of a life; even the taking of one's own life.[67] Yet in the cases mentioned here, the text seems to condone suicide.

## Rabbinic Resolutions

No specific rabbinic passage could be found which deals with Samson's suicide as described in Judg. 16:30. The source below excludes Saul's actions from the realm of forbidden suicide, but makes no mention of Samson. This may imply that the Rabbis condoned Saul's actions but not Samson's.[68] On the other hand, it can be argued that Saul's suicide was deliberately excluded. Since Saul intended to take only his own life, it could be suggested that his suicide was unwarranted—hence the rabbinic exclusion. Since Samson intended to take the lives of the enemy, there was no need to justify his suicide. Hence no specific exclusion was necessary.[69]

| *Bereshit Rabbah* 34:19 | "וְאַךְ" (בר' ט:ה) להביא את החונק עצמו. יכול כשאול? תלמוד לאמר אך. <br><br> The word *ve-akh* (Gen. 9:5) comes to include anyone who commits suicide. Perhaps this also includes someone like Saul? No for the word *akh* delimits.[70] |
|---|---|

67. The Rabbis understood Gen. 9:5 to forbid suicide. See BT *Bava Kamma* 91b, *Bereshit Rabbah* 34:19.

68. See BT *Avodah Zarah* 28a, in which a pagan's desire to kill a Jew at his own expense is compared to Samson killing the Philistines at his own expense.

69. Abravanel, Judg. 16:30, equates Samson's suicide with Saul's. Samson, like Saul feared bodily torture at the hands of the Philistines and acted accordingly. BT *Avodah Zarah* 18a, where Hanina ben Teradion, even under extreme torture, did not take action to shorten his life, does not imply that Saul and Samson sinned in committing suicide to avoid torture. The Talmud does not demand such martyrdom but nonetheless relates Hanina ben Teradion's unusual piety. See Tosafot, *Avodah Zarah* 18a, s.v. *ve-al*; *Gittin* 57b, s.v. *kaftzu*. Cf. also, Ralbag, Judg. 16:24.

70. The word *akh* is usually understood as an exclusionary term. In this exposition, the extra *vav* of *ve-akh* comes to include suicide, while the word *akh* by itself does indeed exclude Saul, given his special circumstance.

## Analysis of Rabbinic Resolutions

The source above offers no explanation for Saul's exclusion. The word *akh* simply excludes Saul from this prohibition.[71] Thus the violation is denied.[72] Justification for the suicide of Saul's arms-bearer does not appear in rabbinic literature.[73] Regarding Ahithophel, the Rabbis did not seek justification for Ahithophel's suicide.[74] He is considered a wicked man who did wicked things.[75]

---

71. For a concise collection of Medieval and modern rabbinic commentary to Saul's actions, see Dov. I. Frimer "Masada in the Light of Halakha" *Tradition* (Summer 1971), pp. 28-36.

72. *Bereshit Rabbah* 34:19 has been understood up to this point to absolve Saul of sin. The following Medieval sources, however, understand this passage differently. *Akh* delimits those who are already given to death such as Hananiah, Mishael and Azariah, Dan. 3:19-23. However, *akh* does not delimit one from actively taking his own life, as Saul did. See Saadiah Gaon, commentary to the Torah, Y. Kapah, Gen. 9:5, *Emunot ve-De'ot* 10:11; see also *Da'at Zekenim mi-Ba'alei Tosafot*, Gen. 9:5. Chaim Shaal, *Petah Enayim, Avodah Zarah* 18a, takes issue with these opinions.

73. Perhaps by analogy, Saul's arms-bearer's actions can find rabbinic justification in the story of the fuller who took his own life upon hearing of Rabbi Judah the Prince's death, BT *Ketuvot* 103b. See Maharsha, ibid., s.v. *mezumman* (end).

74. See Radak, Ralbag, Abravanel, II Sam. 17:23. Ahithophel saw that the tides of the rebellion were turning and that David would defeat Absalom's forces. He also knew David would kill him for following Absalom. He therefore chose suicide rather than face sure death at the hands of David.

75. He is one of six Israelites denied life in the world to come, BT *Sanhedrin* 90a.

# Chapter 14
# Violations in Judges 17-21

The violations in these chapters are not specifically dealt with in this study. Even though the narrator does not explicitly denounce the flagrant violations of Torah law, they are nonetheless hinted at. The text in these chapters stresses three times that in those days there was no king in Israel; everyone did as they pleased.[76] The purpose of these chapters thus seems to be to show how life can degenerate if there is no fear of the king.[77] Therefore, since the text itself implicitly notes wrongdoing, rabbinic response acknowledging guilt was not necessary. For this reason, these violations are not addressed in this study.

---

76. "In those days there was no king in Israel." (Judg. 18:1, 19:1), "In those days there was no king in Israel; everyone did as they pleased" (ibid. 21:25).

77. See Y. Elizur, *Daʾat Mikra* [Hebrew], Jerusalem, 1976; Introduction to Judges 17-21 pp. 156-157.

# Chapter 15
# Violation of Priestly Laws

| Torah | |
|---|---|
| Exod. 28:2, 6, 40 | Make sacral vestments for your brother, Aaron for dignity and adornment. They shall make the ephod of blue, purple and crimson yarns, and of fine twisted linen, worked into designs. And for Aaron's sons also you shall make tunics, and make sashes for them, and make turbans for them for dignity and adornment. |

| Prophets | |
|---|---|
| I Sam. 2:18 | Samuel was engaged in the service of the Lord as an attendant, girded with a linen ephod. |
| Ibid. 22:18 | And Doeg the Edomite went and struck down the priests himself; that day he killed eighty-five men who wore the linen ephod. |
| II Sam. 6:14 | David was girt with a linen ephod. |

### Description of Violations

According to the Torah, the linen ephod was only worn by Aaron, the High Priest, while Aaron's sons, ordinary priests, wore only four garments which did not include the ephod (see Mishnah, *Yoma* 7:5). Yet Samuel and David wore the linen ephod. In addition, the text tolerates eighty-five priests wearing the ephod at once. Surely there could be only one High Priest at a given time!

| Rabbinic Resolution | |
|---|---|
| **Targum Jonathan** I Sam. 2:18 | ושמואל משמש קדם ה' עולימא אסיר כרדוט דבוץ<br><br>Samuel was engaged in the service of the Lord, as an attendant girded with a tunic with sleeves of fine linen. |
| **Targum Jonathan** I Sam 22:18 | ואסתחר דואג אדומאה ושלט הוא בכהניא וקטל ביומא ההוא תמנן וחמשא גברין דכשרין למלבש אפוד דבוץ.<br><br>And Doeg the Edomite went and struck down the priests himself, that day he killed eighty-five men worthy of wearing the linen ephod. |
| JT *Sanhedrin* 10:2 (38a) | ויסב דואג האדמי ויפגע בכהנים וגו' (ש"א כב:יח) לא כן! תני ר' חייא אין ממנין שני כהנים גדולים כאחת. אלא מלמד שהיו כולם ראויין להיות כהנים גדולים.<br><br>"And Doeg the Edomite went and struck down the priests himself, that day he killed eighty-five men who wore the linen ephod" (I Sam. 22:18). But this is not so,[78] for R. Hiyya taught, we don't choose two High Priests to minister at one time. Rather this teaches that they were all worthy of being High Priests. |
| **Targum Jonathan** II Sam. 6:14 | ודוד אסיר כרדוט דבוץ<br><br>David was girt with a tunic with sleeves of fine linen.[79] |

---

78. That eighty-five priests can be wearing the linen ephod at the same time.
79. The parallel passage in I Chron. 15:27 replaces the linen ephod with a *me'il butz*, "robe of fine linen." Targum's rendition of *kardut de-butz* in II Sam 6:14 is thus a translation of the words in Chron (*me'ilim* in II Sam 13:18 is translated as *kardutim*). See Leivy Smolar and Moses Aberbach, *Studies in Targum Jonathan to the Prophets* I: The Halacha in Targum Jonathan (KTAV, 1983), pp. 23-24.

## Analysis of Rabbinic Resolution

Targum Jonathan to 1 Sam. 2:18 and 2 Sam. 6:14 indicate that Samuel and David never wore the linen ephod worn exclusively by the High Priest. They instead wore a linen tunic which resembled the ephod. Thus the violation is denied. Targum Jonathan to 1 Sam. 22:18 and 2:14 explain that the eighty-five priests of Nob were worthy of being High Priests, and relate this by saying that they were worthy of wearing the linen ephod. Since more than one High Priest could not minister at the same time, this means that only one priest actually did wear the linen ephod, and thus the violation is denied.[80]

---

80. Medieval commentators explain that these eighty-five priests did indeed wear the linen ephod, as did Samuel and David. See Radak and Abravanel, I Sam 22:18. However, a close comparison of the three renditions of Targum Jonathan shows that according to rabbinic literature all the priests did not actually wear the linen ephod of the High Priests. This is also the plain meaning of R. Hiyya, JT *Sanhedrin* 10:2 (38a).

# Chapter 16
# Violations Regarding Sacrifice

| Torah | |
|---|---|
| **Lev. 1:3** | If his offering is a burnt offering from the herd, he shall make his offering a male without blemish. He shall bring it to the entrance of the Tent of Meeting. |

| Prophets | |
|---|---|
| **I Sam. 6:14** | The cart came into the field of Joshua of Beth-Shemesh and it stopped there. They split up the wood of the cart and presented the cows as a burnt offering to the Lord. |

## Description of Violation

The Torah states that a male is to be offered as a burnt offering in the Tent of Meeting. The people of Beth-Shemesh violate the law by offering females as burnt offerings outside the Tent of Meeting. And yet the text tolerates both these violations.

| Rabbinic Resolutions | |
|---|---|
| BT *Avodah Zarah* 24b (#1) | מיתיבי ואת הפרות העלו עולה לה' (ש"א ו:יד).<br>הוראת שעה היתה. הא נמי מסתברא דאי לא תימא<br>הכי עולה נקבה מי איכא?<br><br>An objection was raised, "And the cows they offered as burnt offerings to God" (I Sam. 6:14). This was a special ruling [*hora'at sha'ah*] for the occasion.[81] Common sense, indeed, proves it; for had not that been the case, how could a female be used as a burnt offering? |
| BT *Avodah Zarah* 24b (#2) | מנין לעולה נקבה שהיא כשרה בבמת יחיד?<br><br>Whence can it be deduced that a female is fit as a burnt offering on a private shrine? |
| BT *Zevahim* 112b | באו לשילה נאסרו הבמות באו לנב וגבעון הותרו הבמות.<br><br>When they came to Shiloh shrines were forbidden. When they came to Nob and Gibeon, shrines were permitted. |

---

81. Rashi: "Due to miracle performed through the cattle" (s.v. *hora'at sha'ah*).

## Analysis of Rabbinic Resolution

BT *Avodah Zarah* 24b (#1) explains that females were fit for burnt offerings as a case of *horaat shaah*. BT *Avodah Zarah* 24b (#2) indicates that since the shrine at Beth-Shemesh was a private shrine, females were fit as burnt offerings on it.[82] According to this passage the violation is denied. It is also taken for granted in this passage that private shrines at that time were permitted, and BT *Zevahim* 112b corroborates this assumption.[83]

---

82. The Talmud derives this from I Sam. 7:9 and not from this case itself. Often, the Rabbis use the case at hand itself, to show that it was permitted. See for instance ch. 12,

83. A careful reading of this passage reveals that shrines were forbidden until the Tent of Meeting was brought to Nob and Gibeon. At the time of this offering, the Tent of Meeting had not yet come to Nob and Gibeon. The Rabbis, nonetheless, took it for granted that shrines were at this time permitted, as indicated in BT *Avodah Zarah* 24b (#2). Even if BT *Zevahim* 112b is read so closely, as to forbid shrines after the destruction of Shiloh, until the Tent of Meeting was moved to Gibeon and Nob, *Avodah Zarah* 24b (#1) calls I Sam. 6:14 a *horaat shaah*. This would explain the use of animals of Philistines for sacrifices, the use of females for burnt offerings, as well as the offering of sacrifices outside the Tent of Meeting.

# Chapter 17

# Ignorance of the Command to Appoint a King

| Torah | |
|---|---|
| Deut. 17:14-15 | If, when you have entered the land that the Lord your God has given you and occupied it settled in it, you decide, "I will set a king over me, as do all the nations about me," you shall set a king over yourself, one chosen by the Lord your God. |

| Prophets | |
|---|---|
| I Sam. 8:5-7 | And they said to him... appoint a king for us to govern us like all other rations. Samuel was displeased that they said, "Give us a king to govern us." Samuel prayed to the Lord, and the Lord replied to Samuel, "Heed the demand of the people in everything they say to you. For it is not you that they have rejected; it is Me they have rejected as their King." |

### Description of Violation

The Torah commands the appointment of a king. Yet Samuel's reaction to Israel's demand to fulfill this command is anger. Indeed, God Himself expresses anger at Israel's' desire for a king. The text of Samuel seems to be ignorant of this commandment.

| Rabbinic Resolution | |
|---|---|
| **(1) *Sifrei Devarim* 17:14** [84] | והלא מצוה היא מן התורה לשאול להם מלך שנאמר, שום תשים עליך מלך אשר יבחר ה' אלקיך בו (דב' יז:טו) ולמה נענשו בימי שמואל? מפני שהקדימו על ידן. <br><br> Is it not commanded in the Torah to ask for a king? As is written, "You shall set a king over yourself, one chosen by the Lord your God." If so, why were they punished in the days of Samuel? Because they asked for a king before the appointment time. |
| **(2) Ibid.** [85] | לא בקשו להם מלך אלא להעבידם עבודת כוכבים שנאמר, והיינו גם אנחנו ככל הגויים (ש"א ח:כ) <br><br> Israel requested a king in order to lead them to idol worship, as is written, "And we will be like all the other nations" (I Sam 8:20). |
| **(3) BT *Sanhedrin* 20b (#1)** [86] | זקנים שבדור שאלו כהוגן שנאמר, תנה לנו מלך לשפטינו (ש"א ח:ו) אבל עמי הארץ שבהן קלקלו שנאמר והיינו גם אנחנו ככל הגויים ושפטינו מלכנו ויצא לפנינו (ש"א ח:כ) <br><br> The elders of the generation made a fit request, as is written, "Give us a king to judge us" (I Sam. 8:6). But the vulgar acted unworthy as is written, "That we also may be like all the nations and that our king may judge us and go before us" (I Sam. 8:20). |
| **(4) Ibid.** | לא נאמרה פרשה זו אלא כנגד תרעומתן שנאמר, ואמרת אשימה עלי מלך (דב' יז:טו) <br><br> This chapter was written in anticipation of their future murmurings, as is written, "And you shall say, I will appoint a king over me" (Deut. 17:15). |

---

84. Slight variations in Tosefta *Sanhedrin* 4.3, *Midrash Tannaim*, Deut. 17:14.
85. Slight variation in Tosefta *Sanhedrin* 4:3.
86. Slight variation in *Midrash Tannaim*, Deut. 17:14.

| (5) *Midrash Tannaim*, Deut. 17:14 | הרי משה מודיע להם לישראל מה שהן עתידין לעשות שנאמר, עתה שימה לנו מלך לשפטינו ככל הגוים (ש"א ח:ה). |
|---|---|
| | Moses was informing Israel regarding what they were destined to do, as it is written. "Now appoint a king for us like all other nations" (I Sam. 8:5). |

## Analysis of Rabbinic Resolutions

*Sifrei Devarim* 17:14 (#1) indicates that Samuel was angered at the Israelites' desire for a king before the appointed time. The Israelites did not have a genuine need for a king, and were thus wrong in asking for one.[87] *Sifrei Devarim* 17:14 (#1) and BT *Sanhedrin* 20b (#1) expose the intention of the Israelites in demanding a king. The king's purpose is to maintain faithful observance of the Torah among his people.[88] Yet the Israelites (the entire nation) according to *Sifrei Devarim* 17:14 (#1) or the vulgar Israelites according to BT *Sanhedrin* 20b (#1) reflect a different desire in wanting a king. This unsanctioned desire on the part of Israel angered God and Samuel.

BT *Sanhedrin* 20b (#2) and *Midrash Tannaim*, Deut. 17:14, indicate that God does not want the appointment of a king at all. Rather, Deut. 17:14-20 was written only in light of the divine knowledge that the Israelites were destined to sin in this matter.[89] Therefore, the Torah does not command the appointment of a king, but merely permits it. God was angered that Israel rejected Him as their king,[90] and Samuel was either angered for the same reason, or because they rejected him as their leader.[91]

---

87. See Meiri, BT *Horayot* 11b: Ibn Ezra, R. Bahya, S.D. Luzzatto, *Ha'amek Davar*, Deut. 17:14-15.
88. Isaac Arama, *Akedat Yitzhak*, D.Z. Hoffman, Deut. 17:14.
89. See Abravanel, I Sam. 8 (Jerusalem, 1956), pp. 200-211.
90. "And the Lord replied to Samuel, 'Heed the demands of the people in everything they say to you. For it is not you that they have rejected; it is Me they have rejected as their king'" (I Sam. 8:7).
91. See Chapter 9, note 59.

In summation, according to *Sifrei Devarim* 17:14 (#1 and #2) and BT *Sanhedrin* 20b (#1), Samuel was not ignorant of the laws of the appointment of a king, but was angered by the nature or timing of the request for a king. Thus the apparent ignorance is denied. BT *Sanhedrin* 20b (#2) and *Midrash Tannaim*, Deut. 17:14, indicate that the appointment of a king is not commanded in the Torah. Thus the apparent ignorance is explained away. It is not a favorable situation, and thus Samuel was angered. These answers show that God's and Samuel's anger at the Israelites request for a king do not reflect ignorance of the biblical text.[92]

---

92. Additional answers explaining God's and Samuel's anger abound in medieval and later rabbinic literature. See Ramban, Gen. 49:10, *Derashot ha-Ran* #11, *Keli Yakar*, Deut. 17:14. Maharsha, *Sanhehdrin* 20b, s.v. *ve-khein* (end). See collections of these answers in Manasseh ben Israel's *Concilliator*, New York, 1972, Question 180, pp. 285-289; M. Kookis' article, *"Minnui Melekh Reshut o Hovah"* [Hebrew], *Shma'atin* 10 (1966), pp. 13-23; M. Garsiel's, *"Ha-Mahloket ben Shemuel ve-Yisrael be-She'elat Melekh"* [Hebrew] *Bet Mikra* 87 (1981), pp. 325-343; S. Krasner's *Nahlat Shimon: Samuel* (NY: 1982), ch. 19, pp. 201-211.

# Chapter 18
## Ignorance of Laws Pertaining to a King

| Torah | |
|---|---|
| **Deut. 17:14-19** | You should appoint a king over yourself, one chosen by the Lord your God. Be sure to set as king over yourself, one of your own people; you must not set a foreigner over you, one who is not your kinsman. Moreover, he shall not keep many horses or send people back to Egypt to add to his horses, since the Lord has warned you, "You must not go back that way again." And he shall not have many wives, lest his heart go astray; nor shall he amass silver and gold to excess. When he is seated on his royal throne, he shall have a copy of this Torah written for him by the levitical priests. Let it remain with him and let him read in it all his life, so that he may learn to revere the Lord his God, to observe faithfully every word of the Torah as well as these laws. |

| Prophets | |
|---|---|
| **I Sam. 8:10-17** | This will be the practice of the king who will rule over you: He will take your sons and appoint them as his charioteers and horsemen, and they will serve as runners for his chariots. He will appoint them as his chiefs of thousands and of fifties, or they will have to plow his fields, reap his harvest, and make his weapons and the equipment for his chariots. He will take your daughters as perfumers, cooks, and bakers. He will seize your choice fields, vineyards, and olive groves, and give them to his courtiers. He will take a tenth part of your grain and vintage and give it to his officers and courtiers. He will take your male and female slaves, your choice young men, and your asses, and put them to work for him. He will take a tenth of your flocks, and you shall become his slaves. |

## Description of Discrepancy in Law

The laws concerning a king in I Samuel move well beyond those of the Torah. Samuel makes no mention of the laws of Deuteronomy concerning the king. How do we account for Samuel's apparent ignorance of Torah law regarding a king? And by what authority did Samuel move beyond Torah law?

| Rabbinic Resolution | |
|---|---|
| **(1) BT** *Sanhedrin* **20b** | כל האמור בפרשת מלך, מלך מותר בו.<br><br>All that is set out in the chapter of a king [I Sam. 8] he is permitted to do. |
| **(2) Ibid.** | לא נאמרה פרשה זו אלא כדי לאיים עליהם.<br><br>That chapter [I Sam. 8] was intended only to inspire them with fear. |

## Analysis of Rabbinic Resolution

BT *Sanhedrin* 20b (#1) seems to indicate that all the legal provisions mentioned in I Sam. 8:10-17 were indeed operative.[93] Thus the violation is explained away. BT *Sanhedrin* 20b (#2) indicates that Samuel did not intend for this chapter to be considered law, and only said it in order to scare Israel into withdrawing their request for a king. Thus the violation is denied.

According to both passages, Samuel's objective was to express a negative attitude regarding the appointment of a king by mentioning all his liberties.[94] References to the prohibition and the commandments regarding the *Mishneh Torah* would digress from Samuel's objective. Therefore, Samuel did not mention the laws of the Torah here.[95] BT *Sanhedrin* 20b (#1) doesn't explain how Samuel could move beyond the law of the Torah. BT *Sanhedrin* (#2) of course, doesn't have to.[96]

---

93. See Z.H. Chajes, *Kol Sifrei Maharitz Chajes* (Jerusalem, 1958), vol. 1, ch. 7, pp. 43-49.

94. Even according to BT *Sanhedrin* 20b (#1), Samuel expresses a negative attitude regarding the king.

95. Even if Samuel told the Israelites Torah laws of the king according to the Torah, it wasn't necessary to record what he said in the book of Samuel.

96. See Rambam, *Hilkhot Melakhim* 3:8. See also S. Krasner's *Nahalat Shimon: Joshua*, ch. 6, pp. 53-56, Rambam, *ibid.* ch. 4 allows a king all the liberties mentioned in I Sam. 8:10-17. These sources explain that the special rights of a king are based on a social contract made in the days of Joshua between the leaders and his people. On these grounds, Samuel moved beyond what the Torah commands regarding a king.

# Chapter 19

# Violation Relating to Divination

| Torah | |
|---|---|
| **Lev. 19:26** | You shall not practice divination[97] or soothsaying. |

| Prophets | |
|---|---|
| **I Sam. 14:8-10** | Jonathan said, "We will cross over to those men and let them see us. If they say to us, "Wait until we get to you," then we will stay where we are and not go up to them. But if they say, "Come up to us," then we will go up, for the Lord is delivering them into our hands. That shall be our sign. |

### Description of Violation

According to the rabbinic definitions of divination, the Torah prohibits a person from basing his actions on omens. Jonathan seems to be doing just that, by basing his plan of attack on an omen.

---

97. Definitions of "divination" are given as follows:
   a. "Those who practice divination by moles or by fowls or by the stars" (*Sifra* 6:2, BT *Sanhedrin* 66a; *Sanhedrin* adds "or by fish").
   b. "What is divination? One who says, 'My bread fell from my mouth, my staff from my hand, a snake passed my right side, or a fox passed my left side, or a deer crossed my path... [it is an evil omen]'" (*Sifrei Devarim* 18:10 §171).

| Rabbinic Resolution | |
|---|---|
| BT *Hullin* 95b | כל נחש שאינו כאליעזר עבד אברהם (בר' כד:יד) וכיונתן בן שאול (ש"א יד:ט) אינו נחש. <br><br> An omen which is not after the form pronounced by Eliezer, Abraham's servant (Gen. 24:14), or by Jonathan, son of Saul (I Sam. 14:9), is not considered a divination. |

**Analysis of Rabbinic Resolution**

The Talmud seems to admit that Jonathan violated the prohibition against divination. Thus the violation is acknowledged.[98]

---

98. Usually the Rabbis try to justify the actions of a biblical figure who is considered righteous. Occasionally, however, the Rabbis admit that a righteous person did indeed sin (See E. Margoliyot *Ha-Hayyavim b'Mikra ve-Zakka'im b'Talmud u-v'Midrashim* [Hebrew], [London, 1949], introduction). However, when such is the case, the Rabbis sought some type of hidden reaction to the sin in the test (see chaps. 10, 23). When Israel sinned, especially at war, God's providence was withdrawn from them (see for example Num. 14:40-45; above ch. 3; *Sefer ha-Hinnukh* [Jerusalem, 1958], comm. 566, 567, p. 338, reasons behind these commandments). If Jonathan sinned, why didn't the Rabbis seek some type of reference in the text to this sin, and why was Jonathan rewarded with the stunning victory described in I Sam. 14:12-14, as a direct result of this sin? These questions may have led many post-rabbinic commentators to absolve Jonathan of sin, and to explain that our source itself never meant to accuse Jonathan of sinning.

It is difficult to determine this intention of Jonathan from the text. Tosafot, *Hullin* 95b, s.v. *ve-kavvanatan* states that Jonathan acted only to influence his lad. His actions do qualify as divination, as the Talmud states. However, since his intention was to meet the Philistines regardless of what they would say, he did not sin.

Rambam, *Hilkhot Akum* 11:4, states that a divination such as that made by Eliezer is forbidden. *Kesef Mishneh*, ad loc., explains that Rambam omitted Jonathan, either because his text of the Talmud did not list Jonathan along with Eliezer, or because Rambam agrees with Tosafot's opinion that Jonathan acted only to influence his lad. Raavad also absolves Jonathan of sin. The Talmud, he states, merely relates the type of condition which is in violation of divination. The actual conditions themselves which are forbidden can be found in *Sifra*, *Sifrei*, and BT *Sanhedrin* 66a. See also Meiri, *Sanhedrin* 65b, Radak, I Sam. 14:9, Abravanel, Deut. 18:10.

R. Nissim, *Hullin* 95b, explains that if there is good cause, then there is no violation of divination. As the Talmud states, the type of conditions made by Jonathan constitute those which violate the prohibition of divination. However, Jonathan's specific conditions did not violate the Torah. Jonathan merely wanted to see if the Philistines feared that many Israelites were lying in wait. If they would call Jonathan towards them, this would be a sign that they feared a hidden attack. Jonathan would use this knowledge as a strategic asset to help two courageous fighters defeat twenty timorous enemy fighters. The examples of *Sifra*, *Sifrei* and *Sanhedrin* are all irrelevant events that can only be based on belief in evil omens. See also Judah Loew, *Gur Aryeh*, Gen. 24:11.

# Chapter 20

# Reason for Saul Wanting to Put Jonathan to Death

| Torah | |
|---|---|
| Exod. 20:13 | You shall not murder. |

| Prophets | |
|---|---|
| I Sam. 14:43-44 | Saul said to Jonathan, "Tell me what have you done?" And Jonathan told him, "I only tasted a bit of honey with the tip of the stick in my hand. I am ready to die." Saul said, "This and more may God do; you shall be put to death, Jonathan." |

### Description of Violation

There appears to be no precedent in the Torah justifying Saul's wish to have Jonathan put to death. Even if Jonathan transgressed the biblical law of violating an oath, this is not a capital offense. How are Saul's actions to be explained?

| Rabbinic Resolutions | |
|---|---|
| *Tanhuma Vayyeshev 2* [99] | תדע לך כח החרם ... ועוד הוא למוד בן קיש שאמר ארור האיש אשר יאכל לחם עד הערב ונקמתי מאויבי. ולא טעם כל העם לחם ויונתן לא שמע בהשביע אביו את העם וישלח את קצה המטה אשר בידו ויטבול אותה ביערת הדבש וגו' (ש"א יד:כד-כז) ראה שאול פלשתים מתגברים על ישראל וידע שמעלו בחרם. הגיש האפוד וראה שאבן שבט בנימין מכהה אורה. הפיל גורל בינו ובין יונתן בנו ונלכד יונתן. נטל עליו חרב להרגו.<br><br>We also learn the severity of a ban from Saul son of Kish who said, "Cursed be the man who eats any food before night falls and I take revenge on my enemies." So none of the troops ate anything. Jonathan had not heard his father adjure the troop. So he put out the stick he had with him, dipped it into the beehive of honey... (I Sam. 14:24-27). Saul saw the Philistines prevailing over Israel. He knew that they had broken faith with the ban. He brought in the ephod and saw the stone of the tribe of Benjamin was dim. He chose lots between himself and his son, Jonathan, and Jonathan was chosen. He lifted his sword to kill him. |

## Analysis of Rabbinic Resolution

This source indicates that Saul had the right to put Jonathan to death because of the severity of the ban.[100] According to the Midrash, Saul saw that Israel must have sinned in some way because the Philistines were prevailing over

---

99. This passage is found also in *Pirkei de-Rabbi Eliezer* 38 and *Bereshit Rabbati* 38:30, p. 182.
100. See I Sam. 14:42-44 regarding the ban which Jonathan violated. The biblical authority of a ban is brought to light by Ramban (Lev. 27:29), where the case of Jonathan's violation of the ban is addressed.

REASON FOR SAUL WANTING TO PUT JONATHAN TO DEATH

Israel,[101] and that God was not answering their call (I Sam. 14:37). He felt that the only way to defeat the Philistines would be to eradicate the sin from Israel. Thus he was justified in acting this way, and the violation is denied.

---

101. This is the claim of the passage. It is difficult to find where the Philistines prevailed over Israel after the ban was proclaimed. Perhaps this refers to the end of I Sam. 14:31, where the people grew very faint.

# Chapter 21:
## Violation of Proper Judicial Procedure

| Torah | |
|---|---|
| **Deut. 17:6** | A person shall be put to death only on the testimony of two or more witnesses; he must not be put to death on the testimony of single witness. |

| Prophets | |
|---|---|
| **I Sam. 14:43-44** | Saul said to Jonathan, "Tell me what you have done?" And Jonathan told him, "I only tasted a bit of honey with the tip of my stick in my hand. I am ready to die." Saul said, "Thus and more may God do: you shall be put to death, Jonathan." |

### Description of Violation

Torah law allows for capital punishment only when a criminal is convicted by the testimony of two witnesses. How then was Saul prepared to kill Jonathan in the absence of the testimony of two or more witnesses?

| Rabbinic Resolution | |
|---|---|
| **Tanhuma, Vayyeshev 2** [102] | הגיש האפוד וראה שאבן שבט בנימין מכהה אורה. הפיל גורל בינו ובין יונתן בנו ונלכד יונתן.<br><br>He saw on the ephod that the stone of the tribe of Benjamin was dim. He chose lots between him and Jonathan, and Jonathan was chosen. |

102. A similar account appears in *Pirkei de-Rabbi Eliezer* 38, *Bereshit Rabbati*, Gen. 38:30, p. 187.

## Analysis of Rabbinic Resolution

According to our source, no testimony was needed, for a divine oracle procedure convicted Jonathan. Thus the violation is denied.[103]

---

103. Cf. the discussions of Joshua killing Achan on his own admission (above ch. 4), and David killing the Amalekite lad on his own admission (below ch. 28). The lists of *horàat shàah* of *Encyclopedia Talmudit*, Jerusalem 1957, vol. 8, columns 512-517, and of Z. H. Chajes, *Horàat Shàah* [Hebrew], Jerusalem, 1958, vol. I, pp. 23-43, include Joshua's and David's actions in their lists of *horàot shàah*. Yet both lists omit Saul's readiness to have Jonathan killed without testimony. Perhaps Saul's actions are not included as an act of *horàat shàah*, because, in fact, Saul did not kill Jonathan. Cf. also Rambam, *Hilkhot Sanhedrin* 18:6.

# Chapter 22
## Violations of Genealogy Laws
## and of the Law Excluding Non-Israelites
## From Serving as King

| Torah | |
|---|---|
| **Deut. 17:15** | You shall appoint a king over yourself, one chosen by the Lord your God. Be sure to set as king over you, one of your own people. You must not set a foreigner over you, one who is not your kinsman. |
| **Deut. 23:4** | No Ammonite or Moabite shall be admitted into the congregation of the Lord, none of his descendants, even in the tenth generation shall be admitted into the congregation of the Lord. |

| Prophets | |
|---|---|
| **(1) I Sam. 16:1** | And the Lord said to Samuel... fill your horn with oil and set out; I am sending you to Jesse the Bethlehemite, for I have decided on one of his sons to be king. |
| **(2) I Kings 14:21** | Rehoboam son of Solomon had become king in Judah... his mother's name was Naamah the Ammonitess.[104] |

---

104. The biblical text condemns Solomon's marriages to foreign women (see I Kings 11:1-5). This section deals with the genealogy of Rehoboam, and how he was able to serve as king.

## Description of Violations

The Torah forbids the appointment of a king from a foreign nation.[105] Ammonites, Moabites, and their descendants can never marry into the Israelite nation. Therefore David, a descendant of Ruth the Moabite, and Rehoboam, son of Naamah the Ammonite, could not be admitted into our congregation, and they are unfit to serve as king.

| Rabbinic Resolutions | |
|---|---|
| **(1) BT *Yevamot* 76b** | עמוני ומואבי אסורים ואיסרון איסור עולם, אבל נקיבותיהם מותרות מיד. <br><br> An Ammonite and a Moabite are forbidden to enter the congregation of the Lord, and their prohibition is forever. Their women, however, are permitted immediately after conversion (to marry an Israelite). |
| **(2) Ibid. 77a** | אמר דוד לפני הקב"ה, רבונו של עולם שני מוסרות שהיו עלי פתחתם. רות המואביה ונעמה העמונית. <br><br> David said to God, O Master of the world: Two bonds were fastened to me,[106] and You loosened them: Ruth the Moabite and Naamah the Ammonite. |

## Analysis of Rabbinic Resolutions

BT *Yevamot* 76b indicates that the prohibition against Ammonites and Moabites does not apply to females. *Yevamot* 77a does not address the Torah law specifically, yet allows for David's and Rehoboam's acceptance into the congregation as well as the kingship. Thus, according to both passages the violation is denied.

---

105. David's great-grandmother, Ruth, was of Moabite stock. Rehoboam's mother, as I Kings 14:21 indicates, was of Ammonite stock. The Torah considers all the descendants of Moabites and Ammonites to have the same status; see Deut. 23:4.
106. Upon David's dynasty, threatening the legitimacy of his kingdom.

# Chapter 23

## Violation of Possessing a Graven Image

| Torah | |
|---|---|
| **Exod. 20:4** | You shall not make for yourself a sculptured image, or any likeness of what is in the heavens above, or on the earth below, or in the waters under the earth. |

| Prophets | |
|---|---|
| **I Sam. 19:13** | Michal then took the teraphim,[107] laid it on the bed, and covered it with a cloth, and at its head she put a net of goat's hair. |

### Description of Violation

Graven images are forbidden by the Torah.[108] The teraphim that Michal placed in David's bed seem to be graven images in the form of a man.[109] Yet the text tolerates this apparent violation of Torah law.

---

107. Teraphim is an object of reverence to Laban (Gen. 31:19), a means of divination (Ezek. 21:26, Zech. 10:2), and is condemned in I Sam. 15:23, II Kings 23:24. Usage of teraphim in these contexts is enough to raise a question about its appearance in David's house. The objection in this chapter comes from the obvious resemblance of teraphim to graven images.

108. The Rabbis do not distinguish between "making" an idol or "possessing" one.

109. Targum Jonathan reads *tzalmanayya* (*tzelem* means "image").

## Rabbinic Resolution

Rabbinic resolution to this apparent violation could not be found. Thus, this violation falls under the category, "Violation Ignored."[110]

---

110. Post-rabbinic material abounds on the contradiction of the righteous David having teraphim in his house. Yosef Kara, I Sam. 19:13, Ibn Ezra, Gen. 31:19, Radak and Ralbag, I Sam. 19:13, explain away the problem of idolatry, yet they introduce a new problem of divination. Abravanel explains that some women kept images of their husbands and argues that since this image was not used for idolatry or divination, it is permitted. This explanation is problematic, however, in light of the fact that the text calls them teraphim. Isaac Acosta, I Sam 19:13, explains that any image which resembles the image of a human, even in size, can be called teraphim. Thus the word is used in this context. See Ibn Ezra and Radak, Hosea 3:4.

# Chapter 24

## Violation of the Law of Murder

| Torah | |
|---|---|
| Exod. 23:7 | Do not bring death on the innocent. |

| Prophets | |
|---|---|
| I Sam. 25:5, 8, 10-11, 13,22 | David dispatched ten young man and instructed them, "Go up to Carmel... when you come to Nabal... say as follows.... Please give your servants and your son David whatever you can." Nabal answered David's servants, "Who is David.... Should I then take my bread and my water and the meat that I slaughtered... and give them to men who come from I don't know where?... and David said to his men, "Gird your swords... may God do thus and more to the enemies of David if, by the light of the morning, I leave a single man of his." |

### Description of Violation

Nabal, despite his stinginess, certainly did not incur the death penalty. His men all the more so were not guilty of a capital offense. What was the basis of David's readiness to kill all these people?

| Rabbinic Resolutions | |
|---|---|
| **BT** *Megillah* **14b** [111] | אמר לה מורד במלכות הוא ולא צריך למידייניה. אמרה לו עדיין שאול קיים ולא יצא טבעך בעולם. אמר לה, ברוך טעמך וברוכה את אשר כליתני היום הזה מבוא בדמים והושע ידי לי (ש"א כה:לג).<br><br>David said to Abigail, "He [Nabal] is a rebel against the king and no trial is necessary for him." She replied, "Saul is still alive and your fame is not yet spread abroad in the world." Then he said to her, "Blessed be your prudence and blessed be yourself for restraining me from seeking redress in blood by my own hands" (I Sam. 25:33). |
| *Midrash Tehillim* **53:1** | טובה היתה אביגיל לדוד מכל הקרבנות שבעולם. שאילו עשה אותו מעשה שחשב לעשות לנבל, אילו היה מקריב כל הקרבנות שבעולם, לא היו מכפרים לו והיא באתה אליו ומלטתהו. אמרה לו אביגיל לדוד, אדוני המלך אם בא הדין הזה אליך מה אתה עושה? אם ילך עני ויאמר לבעל הבית עשה עמי צדקה, תן לי פת אחד, ואינו נזקק לו, והעני נופל עליו והרגו, אם הם באים אצלך לדין מה אתה עושה? ואתה מפקפק בדבר ואין אתה יכול להוציאו, והן אומרים לא עשה כן לנבל? אל תאמר בשביל שאתה מלך אין אדם מוכיחני. הוכח אתה בעצמך.<br><br>Abigail was better for David than all the sacrifices in the world, for if David had carried out his intentions with Nabal, he would not have been forgiven even if he offered all the sacrifices in the world, and Abigail came to save him. She said to David, "My Lord the king, if the following case came to you, how would you rule? If a man refused to give charity or food to a poor person who asked for it, and because of the refusal the poor person killed him, how would you rule? And as you hesitate in your ruling, they would say, "Did he not do the same to Nabal?" And do not say because you are king, "No one can rebuke me for doing it," rebuke yourself for it."[112] |

111. Also found in *Midrash Shmuel* 23:12.
112. A reminder of the Talmudic phrase, BT *Sanhedrin* 18a: *hitkosheshu ve-kashu*

## Analysis of Rabbinic Resolutions

According to BT *Megillah* 14b, David justifies his actions because of his special rights as king. Samuel had already anointed him (I Sam. 16:13) and David considered Nabal a rebellious subject. Abigail agrees that had Nabal refused the king he would have been guilty of a capital offense. David, however, Abigail argued, was not yet king because Saul was still king. David did not have the right to kill Nabal. Thus, according to this passage, had David carried out his intentions, he would have transgressed the law by killing the innocent. Thus, in theory the violation is acknowledged.

According to *Midrash Tehillim* 53:1, David's kingship is not questioned.[113] Even as king, David would have transgressed Torah law by killing Nabal and his men.[114] According to *Megillah* 14b, which differs on this point, had David been king, he would have been justified in killing Nabal.[115] Thus, in theory again, the violation is acknowledged.

---

*keshat atzmekha ve-ahar kakh keshat aherim.* Through a play on words, this passage means rebuke yourself before rebuking others. This parable, attributed to Abigail, resembles the parable of Nathan in II Sam. 12:1-4.

113. David's position as king is stressed twice by Abigail in this passage. *Yalkut's* paraphrase of this passage, 2:134, does not have Abigail mentioning David's kingship. Perhaps this was done to conform to the Talmudic opinion that David was not considered a king in Saul's lifetime.

114. Neither passage questions David's readiness to kill Nabal's men. Perhaps as king, David felt they all deserved to die for not objecting to Nabal's stinginess. See Ralbag, I Sam. 25:22, Malbim, I Sam. 25:17.

115. For a discourse on the special rights of a king see Z.H. Chajes, *Kol Sifrei Mahartiz Chajes*, vol. I, pp. 43-49; Y. Gershuni, *Kol Tzofayikh*, pp. 168-170.

# Chapter 25

# Violation of Laws Relating to Marriage Relationship

| Torah | |
|---|---|
| **Exod. 20:13** | You shall not commit adultery. |
| **Deut. 24:1-4** | A man takes a wife and possesses her. She fails to please him and he writes her a bill of divorce.... She leaves his household and becomes the wife of another man, then this latter man rejects her and writes her a bill of divorce... and sends her away from his house, or the man who married her last dies. Then the first husband who divorced her shall not take her to wife again since she has been defiled. |

| Prophets | |
|---|---|
| **I Sam. 18:27** | Saul then gave him [David] his daughter Michal to marriage. |
| **Ibid 25:44** | Saul had given his daughter Michal, David's wife to Palti, son of Laish, from Galim. |
| **II. Sam. 3:14-15** | David sent messengers to Ish-bosheth, son of Saul, saying, "Give me my wife, Michal for whom I paid the bride price of one hundred Philistines foreskins." So Ish-bosheth sent, and had her taken from her husband, Paltiel son of Laish. |

## Description of Violations

The Torah forbids adultery and also forbids a man to remarry a former wife who had, since their divorce, been married to another man. Palti ben Laish and Michal seem to violate the first law, and David, the second.

| Rabbinic Resolutions | |
|---|---|
| **BT *Sanhedrin* 19b (#1)** | אמר ליה, אי בעית דאתן לך מיכל, זיל אייתי לי מאה ערלות פלשתים. אזל אייתי ליה. אמר ליה מלוה ופרוטה אית לך גבאי. שאול סבר מלוה ופרוטה דעתיה אמלוה. ודוד סבר מלוה ופרוטה דעתיה אפרוטה. ואי בעת אימא דכולי עלמא מלוה ופרוטה דעתיה אפרוטה, שאול סבר לא חזו ולא מידי ודוד סבר חזו לכלבי ושונרי |
| | Saul said to David, "If you wish me to give you Michal to wife, go and bring me a hundred foreskins of the Philistines." He went and brought them to him. Then he said, "You have now two claims on me, the repayment of a loan[116] and a *perutah*."[117] Saul held that when a loan and a *perutah* are offered [as *kiddushin*] he [the would-be husband] thinks mainly of the loan,[118] but in David's view, when there is a loan and a *perutah*, the mind is set on the *perutah*.[119] Alternatively, all agree that where a loan and a *perutah* are offered the mind is set on the *perutah*.[120] Saul, however, thought that the hundred foreskins had no value,[121] while David held that they had value at least as food for dogs and cats.[122] |

116. Saul's promise to enrich David, I Sam. 17:25, stands as a loan (Rashi, *Sanhedrin* 19b, s.v. *milveh u-ferutah*).

117. A *perutah* is sufficient to serve as a token of betrothal (BT *Kiddushin* 2a, Rambam, *Hilkhot Ishut* 3:1).

118. Consequently, she would not be betrothed, for in returning a loan, the debtor is not obliged to return the actual coin lent, but its equivalent. The woman then receives nothing at the time of betrothal, by which it should be effected (see BT *Kiddushin* 6b).

119. Thus the betrothal is valid.

120. This is the decision of the Talmud, BT *Kiddushin* 47a.

121. Thus the betrothal is not valid.

122. Thus the betrothal is valid. Saul's side of the first argument is considered by Tosafot, *Hagigah* 16a, s.v. *Yosi*, to be uncontested. However, Talmudic law in this

| BT *Sanhedrin* 19b (#2) | נעץ חרב בינו לבינה אמר, כל העוסק בדבר זה ידקר בחרב זה....<br><br>שלא טעמו טעם ביאה<br><br>Palti inserted a sword between himself and Michal and said, "Whoever indulges in this thing [marital relations] shall be pierced with this sword." And they did not taste the pleasure of marital relations.[123] |
|---|---|
| *Vayyikra Rabbah* 23:10 | א-ל מעיד עליו שלא נגע באשת דוד.<br><br>God is witness on him that he [Palti] did not go near David's wife.[124] |

## Analysis of Rabbinic Resolutions

According to BT *Sanhedrin* 19b (#1), if David was never really married to Michal, then Palti and Michal did not commit adultery. Thus David also

---

matter sides with David, BT *Kiddushin* 47a. BT *Sanhedrin* 19b (#1) offers that Saul and David agreed on this first point and that their differences lay in whether the hundred foreskins had any value. Tosafot may contend that in this matter as well the law sided with Saul. It is, however, the sentiment of the Talmud that the law sides with David in matters of halachic dispute: *Halakhah kemoto bekhol makom* (BT *Sanhedrin* 93b). Therefore, if we consider David's side of the argument, the three parties are in violation of the Torah laws brought down here. For this reason, BT *Sanhedrin* 19b (#2) and *Vayyikra Rabb*ah 23:10 are preferable justifications for the violations.

123. R. Yosi b. Kipper, BT *Yevamot* 11b, allows for a woman who did not have relations with her second husband to return to her first husband. The law, however, sides with the Rabbis, who say that even in such a case, she is forbidden to her first husband. Thus, even if, as BT *Sanhedrin* 19b (#2) and *Vayyikra Rabbah* 23:10 indicate, Palti and Michal did not have marital relations, David would still have violated the Torah. See Rambam, *Hilkhot Gerushin* 11:13, *Tur, Even ha-Ezer* 10.

124. Maharsha, *Sanhedrin* 19b, states that according to BT *Sanhedrin* 19b (#2), not only did Palti not touch Michal, but he never even married her. He presumably lived with her because this was the order of the king. However, he feared violating a married woman and thus never gave her *kiddushin*. Therefore, David was taking back his own wife. Thus all violations are denied.

did not violate the Torah by taking Michal back, assuming Palti granted Michal a divorce, and the violations are denied.

According to BT *Sanhedrin* 19b (#2) and *Vayyikra Rabbah* 23:10, Palti and Michal never had marital relations. Therefore, Palti and Michal did not commit adultery. And since Michal was not defiled by another man, David did not violate the Torah by taking her back. Thus all violations are denied.

# Chapter 26

# Violation of Proper Burial Procedure

| Torah | |
|---|---|
| **Deut. 21:22-23** | If a man is guilty of a capital offense and is put to death, and you impale him on a stake, you must not let his corpse remain on the stake overnight, but must bury him the same day. |

| Prophets | |
|---|---|
| **I Sam. 31:11-12** | When the inhabitants of Jabesh-gilead heard about what the Philistines had done to Saul, all their stalwart men set out and marched all night, they removed the bodies of Saul and his men from the wall of Beth-shan came to Jabesh and burned them there. |

## Description of Violation

The Torah requires the burial of the dead.[125] Why then does the text tolerate the burning of Saul and his sons by the inhabitants of Jabesh-gilead?

---

125. Deut. 21:23 speaks only of the burial of capital offenders. However, the burial of all dead is included in this law. See BT *Sanhedrin* 46b; Rambam, *Minyan ha-Mitzvot*, pos. comm. #231.

| Rabbinic Resolution | |
|---|---|
| **Targum Jonathan** I Sam. 31:12 | וקמו כל גבר גבר ואזלו כל ליליא ונסיבו ית גופא דשאול וית גופי בנוהי משורא דבית שן ואתי ליבש דקלן על מלכיא תמן. |
| | All the mighty men set out and marched all night, and they removed the bodies of Saul and his sons from the wall of Beth-shan and came to Jabesh and made a royal burning for them then. |

## Analysis of Rabbinic Resolution

According to Targum Jonathan, the bodies of Saul and his sons were not burnt at all. Instead, they performed a common practice at the death of a king. They burned the king's clothes and staff. Thus the violation is denied.[126]

---

126. See also Jer. 34:5; I Chron. 16:14, *ibid.* 21:19. The corresponding verse in Chronicles to I Sam. 31:12 omits the burning of Saul and his sons entirely. See *Studies in Targum Jonathan to the Prophets*, pp. 8-9. Medieval commentators make note of this tradition of Jonathan, yet insist that Saul's and his son's bodies were indeed burned. Their bodies became so infected and infested with worms, they claim that the people of Jabesh-gilead acted correctly in burning them. Then, as v. 13 states, their bones were buried. See Radak, Abravanel, I Sam. 31:12.

# Chapter 27

## Reason for David Wanting
## the Amalekite Lad to be Put to Death

| Torah | |
|---|---|
| Exod. 23:6 | Do not bring death on the innocent. |

| Prophets | |
|---|---|
| II Sam. 1:6-10:16 | The young lad who brought him [David] the news answered, "I happened to be at Mount Gilboa, and I saw Saul leaning on his spear, and the chariots and horsemen closing in on him. He looked around and saw me, and he called to me. When I responded, 'Here I am,' he asked me, 'Who are you?' And I told him that I was an Amalekite. Then he said to me, 'Stand over me, and finish me off for I am in agony and am barely alive.' So I stood over him and finished him off, for I knew that he would never rise from where he was lying...." And David said to him, "Your blood be on your own head. Your own mouth testified against you when you said, 'I put the Lord's anointed to death.'" |

### Description of Violation

There appears to be no precedent in the Torah justifying David's actions in putting the Amalekite lad to death. The lad merely obeyed King Saul, who surely would have died even had the lad not killed him.[127] How are David's actions to be explained?

| Rabbinic Resolutions | |
|---|---|
| **Mekhilta, Amalek 2** | ויאמר דוד אל הנער המגיד לו, אי מזה אתה ויאמר בן איש גר עמלקי אנכי (ש"ב א:יג). נזכר דוד באותה שעה מה שנאמר למשה רבינו, אם יבוא אחד מכל אומות העולם להתגייר שיקבלו אותו, ומביתו של עמלק אל יקבלו אותו. מיד, ויאמר אליו דוד דמך על ראשך כי פיך ענה בך (שם:טז)לכך אמר מדר דר (שמ' יז:טז). <br><br> David said to the lad that told him (of Saul's death) "Who are you?" He answered, "I am the son of an Amalekite convert" (II Sam. 1:13). At that moment, David recalled what had been told to Moses our teacher—that if a person of any nation should desire to convert to Judaism, accept him, but a person from the house of Amalek should not be received. Immediately: "And David said to him, 'Your blood be in your own head. Your own mouth testified against you'" (ibid. 16). Therefore the verse states, "throughout the generations" (Exod. 17:16). |
| **Tanhuma, Ki Teitzei 11** | ויאמר דוד אל הנער המגיד לו, אי מזה אתה, ויאמר בן איש גר עמלקי אנכי (שב"א:יג) בנו של דואג האדומי היה. ויאמר אליו דוד דמיך על ראשך כי פיך וגו' (שם:טז) דמיך כתיב הרבה דמים שפכת, הרגת נוב עיר הכהנים. <br><br> David said to the lad that told him (of Saul's death) "Who are you?" he answered "I am the son of an Amalekite stranger" (II Sam. 1:13). He was the son of Doeg the Edomite. David said, "Your blood be on your own head." "Bloods" is written.[128] Much blood have you shed; you killed the priests of Nob. |

127. The biblical text and rabbinic literature do not condemn Abimelech's lad for killing the near-dead Abimelech (Judg. 9:53-54). The case of the Amalekite lad seems to be the same.

128. The *ketiv* (written form) is in plural, "bloods," דמיך. However the written form is singular, "blood," דמך. The plural of blood is written to signify that this Amalekite lad took part in a mass murder. See however, Radak, II Sam. 1:16. *Tanhuma*, Ki Teitzei, makes use of the *ketiv*.

## Analysis of Rabbinic Resolutions

*Mekhilta*, Amalek, and *Tanhuma*, Ki Teitzei, ignore the textual basis for the Amalekite lad's alleged guilt—for putting the Lord's anointed to death. Perhaps on this basis alone, David was not justified in killing the Amalekite lad.[129] According to *Mekhilta*, Amalek, the lad deserved to die because he was an Amalekite, a people who are biblically doomed to death.[130] This source teaches that even Amalekite converts to Judaism share this fate. Thus the violation is denied. *Tanhuma*, Ki Teitzei, indicates that the Amalekite lad was put to death for his apparent role in the killing of the priests of Nob.[131] Thus the violation is denied.

---

129. See Ralbag and Abravanel, II Sam. 1:14. Cf. also J.L. Ginsberg, *Musar ha-Nevi'im* [Hebrew] (Jerusalem, 1976), vol. II, p. 13 (3).

130. Deut. 25:19. See Rambam, *Hilkhot Melakhim* 5:5, *Hagahot Maimonot*, ad. loc. (א).

131. Rashi, II Sam. 1:2, cites the *Pesikta*, which identifies the Amalekite lad as Doeg, and disagrees.

# Chapter 28

## Violation of Proper Judicial Procedure

| Torah | |
|---|---|
| **Deut. 17:6** | A person shall be put to death only on the testimony of two or more witnesses: he must not be put to death on the testimony of a single witness. |

| Prophets | |
|---|---|
| **II Sam. 1:16** | And David said to him, "Your blood shall be on your own head. Your own mouth testified against you when you said, 'I put the Lord's anointed death.'" |

### Description of Violation

Torah law allows for capital punishment only when a criminal is convicted by the testimony of two witnesses. How then did David kill the Amalekite lad in the absence of the testimony of two or more witnesses?

| | Rabbinic Resolution |
|---|---|
| *Mekhilta,*<br>**Amalek 2** | ויאמר דוד אל הנער המגיד לו, אי מזה אתה ויאמר בן איש גר עמלקי אנכי (ש"ב א:יג). נזכר דוד באותה שעה מה שנאמר למשה רבינו, אם יבוא אחד מכל אומות העולם להתגייר שיקבלו אותו, ומביתו של עמלק אל יקבלו אותו. מיד, ויאמר אליו דוד דמך על ראשך כי פיך ענה בך (שם:טז) לכך אמר מדר דר (שמ' יז:טז). |
| | David said to the lad that told him (of Saul's death) "Who are you?" He answered, "I am the son of an Amalekite convert" (II Sam. 1:13). At that moment, David recalled what had been told to Moses our teacher—that if a person of any nation should desire to convert to Judaism, accept him, but a person from the house of Amalek should not be received. Immediately: "And David said to him, 'Your blood be in your own head. Your own mouth testified against you'" (ibid. 16). Therefore the verse states, "throughout the generations" (Exod. 17:16). |

## Analysis of Rabbinic Resolution

Our source indicates that David killed the lad who finished off Saul because the lad was an Amalekite. Since Amalekites are biblically doomed to death,[132] David was justified in killing the Amalekite lad. Thus the violation is denied.[133]

---

132. Deut. 25:19. See Rambam, *Hilkhot Melakhim* 5:5, *Hagahot Maimonot* ad. loc. (א).

133. Rambam, *Hilkhot Sanhedrin* 18:6, classifies David's having the Amalekite lad put to death on his own admission as *hora'at sha'ah*. David's actions are also classified in the lists of *hora'at sha'ah* of *Encyclopedia Talmudit* (Jerusalem, 1957), vol. 8, cols. 512-517, and of Z.H. Chajes, *Kol Sifrei Maharitz Chajes* [Hebrew] (Jerusalem, 1958), vol. 1, pp. 23-43. See also Ralbag, Abravanel, II Sam. 1:14.

# Chapter 29
# Violation of Priestly Laws

| Torah | |
|---|---|
| **Num. 3:10** | You shall make Aaron and his sons responsible for obeying their priestly duties; any outsider who encroaches shall be put to death.[134] |

| Prophets | |
|---|---|
| **II Sam. 8:18** | And David's sons were priests. |

## Description of Violation

The Torah separates the sons of Aaron from the rest of Israel in their service of God. Performance of priestly duties by an Israelite, not of the sons of Aaron, is a capital offense.[135] How then could David's sons, who were Judites, serve as priests in light of this prohibition?[136]

---

134. See also Numbers 1:51; 3:18; 18:7. BT *Shabbat* 31a emphasizes that the exclusion of non-priests from acting as priests even applies to David, king of Israel.
135. Uzziah, king of Judah, is punished with leprosy for assuming priestly duties in II Chron. 26:16-21. Leprosy is considered close to death (see Num. 12:12, Targum Jonathan to Isa. 6:1).
136. The corresponding passage to II Sam. 8:18 in I Chron. 18:17 reads, "And David's sons were chief officials [*rishonim*]."

| Rabbinic Resolutions | |
|---|---|
| *Mekhilta,* **Yitro 18:1** | כהן מדין רבי אליעזר המודעי אומר שר היה, כענין שנאמר, ובני דוד כהנים היו (ש"ב ח:ח).<br><br>Priest of Midian R. Eliezer of Modiin states, He (Jethro) was an officer, as is stated similarly, and David's sons were officers (II Sam. 8:18).[137] |
| **Targum Jonathan II Sam. 8:18** | ובני דוד רברבין היו<br><br>And David's sons were officers.[138] |
| **BT *Nedarim* 62a** | ובני דוד כהנים היו וכי כהנים היו? אלא מה כהן נוטל בראש אף תלמיד חכם נוטל בראש.<br><br>And David's sons were priests. Were they indeed priests?[139] Rather, just as a priest receive his portion first, so does the scholar.[140] |

## Analysis of Rabbinic Resolution

All three rabbinic sources state that the text never meant to identify David's sons as priests. *Mekhilta* (Yitro) and Targum Jonathan to II Sam.

137. Before this opinion, R. Joshua claims that the definition of the description of Jethro, Hebrew *kohen*, is "sorcerer," as we see in Judg. 18:30, in which *kohen* is given a negative connotation. David's sons (II Sam. 8:18) and Yehonatan's sons (Judg. 18:30) are given the same description of *kohen*. Yet David's sons are given a favorable description in BT *Sanhedrin* 62a. This description appears in Judges 17-19, a portion not dealt with in this study. Although no direct indication is given that the law is violated in these chapters, an impression of sinfulness is nonetheless made. See ch. 14.

138. See Rashi, Exod. 19:6. For additional use of kohen meaning "officer," see II Sam. 20:26, Targum Jonathan, Rashi, Radak.

139. The previous clause "Were they indeed priests?" is a gloss inserted by Y. Zirkes, *Hagahot ha-Bah*.

140. The common link between the priest and David's sons is *notel ba-rosh*, receiving a first portion. This link is further strengthened in I Chron. 18:17 where David's sons are called *rishonim*.

8:18 translate *kohen* as "officer," and BT *Nedarim* 62a as "scholar." This last source also explains why, if David's sons were never meant to be designated as priests, the text nevertheless refers to them as such.[141] Thus the violation is denied.

---

141. Targum Jonathan uses three words to describe *kohen*: When the person is truly a *kohen*, then Targum uses *kohen* or *kohanayya*, as in I Sam. 2:35. If the person is an idolatrous priest, then *kumra* is used, as in I Sam. 2:35. If the person is not really a priest at all, then *rav* or *ravravin* is used, as in II Sam. 20:26.

# Chapter 30
# Violation in Seeking the Welfare of Ammonites

| Torah | |
|---|---|
| Deut. 23:7 | You shall never seek their peace nor their [Ammonites and Moabites] benefit as long as you live. |

| Prophets | |
|---|---|
| II Sam. 10:2 | David said, "I will show kindness to Hanun, son of Nahash as his father showed kindness to me." And David sent his courtiers to comfort him over his father. |

### Description of Violation

Torah law forbids seeking the peace of, or dealing kindly with, Ammon and Moab. David seems to go out of his way to do something the Torah prohibits, without any mention in the narrative of any wrongdoing.

| Rabbinic Resolution | |
|---|---|
| *Tanhuma,* **Pinehas 3** [142] | אמר לו הקב"ה, אתה תעבור על דברי? אני כתבתי ולא תדרוש לשלומם (דב' כג:ז) ואת עושה עמם גמילת חסד? ... סוף בא לידי בזיון... ובא לידי מלחמה. |
| | God said to David, "Will you transgress my word? I wrote, 'You shall not seek their peace' (Deut. 23:7), and you show kindness to them?"... In the end he came unto disgrace... and unto war. |

---

142. A parallel passage appears at *Bemidbar Rabbah* 21:6.

## Analysis of Rabbinic Resolution

No resolution is provided,[143] not even the customary last resort of *hora'at sha'ah*, but the violation is acknowledged.[144]

---

143. Usually, the Rabbis try to justify any act of a biblical figure who is considered righteous. Occasionally, however, the Rabbis resolve an unnoticed violation with the answer that the person did wrong, even if the person is considered righteous. See E. Margaliot, *Ha-Hayyavim b'Mikra ve-Zakkaim b'Talmud u-v'Midrashim* [Hebrew] (London, 1949), introduction.

144. In medieval and later rabbinic literature, halakhic justification for David's action abound. See R. Eliezer of Metz, *Sefer Yere'im*, §250, p. 226, and all commentaries there, especially A.A. Schiff's *To'afot Re'em*. See also R. Shlomo Zalman, *Toldot Adam*, vol. 2, p. 44. In addition, see Rambam, *Hilkhot Melakhim* 6:6, and *Kesef Mishneh*, *Hagahot Maimonot*, and *Or Sameah*, *ad loc*. The verse prohibits *seeking* the peace of the Ammonites. David did *not seek* their peace. He responded to their good gesture to him.

# Chapter 31

# Violation Relating to the
# Punishment for Stealing and Slaughtering Sheep

| Torah | |
|---|---|
| Exod. 21:37 | When a man steals an ox or a sheep, and slaughters it or sells it, he shall pay five oxen for the ox, and four sheep for the sheep. |

| Prophets | |
|---|---|
| II Sam. 12:4-6 | One day a traveler came to the rich man, but he was loath to take anything from his own flocks or herds to prepare a meal for the guest who had come to him; so he took the poor man's lamb and prepared it for the man who had come to him. David flew into a rage against the man, and said to Nathan, "As the Lord lives, the man who did this deserves to die. He shall pay for the lamb four times over, because he did such a thing and showed no pity." |

### Description of Violation

David reflects some knowledge of Torah law of stealing and slaughtering sheep by demanding the fourfold restitution. However, the Torah does not consider this a capital offense. The execution of David's ruling would have violated Torah law. How can David's actions be explained?[145]

---

145. According to rabbinic law, when a capital punishment as well as a monetary punishment are incumbent or a person for the same crime, the lesser punishment,

## Rabbinic Resolution

No rabbinic resolution could be found which addresses David's stringent ruling. Had this been a real case and this ruling been executed, it would have been a miscarriage of justice and a violation of Torah law.[146] Thus, the violation is ignored.

---

the monetary one, is dropped. See BT *Ketuvot* 30b. David violates this law. In general, rabbinic literature seeks to resolve not only Torah violations by righteous biblical characters, but rabbinic violations as well. This study, however, deals only with violations of Torah law.

146. Post-rabbinic resolutions to David's overly stringent ruling include the following:

- Rashi and Yosef Kara to II Sam. 12:5 explain that David never meant for the sheep-stealer to die. Rather, *ben mavet* means a person worthy of dying (see Ibn Ezra, Exod. 21:29, s.v. *ve-gam ba'alav yumat*).
- Abravanel explains that the overly cruel actions of the rich man are so horrible that they actually warrant the death penalty.
- Malbim explains David's ruling in light of his special right as king to correct a situation as he sees fit.

Thus, according to Rashi, the violation is denied. According to Abravanel, the violation is explained away. And according to Malbim, David's actions would fall under the category of *hora'at sha'ah*. For further reading on a king's special rights, see Rambam, *Hilkhot Melakhim* 3:10, *Hilkhot Rotze'ah* 2:4; and see *Kol Sifrei Mahartiz Chajes* (Jerusalem, 1958), vol. 1, pp. 43-49.

# Chapter 32
# Violation of Incest Laws

| Torah | |
|---|---|
| Lev. 18:9 | The nakedness of your sister—your father's daughter or your mother's, whether born into the household or outside—do not uncover their nakedness.[147] |

| Prophets | |
|---|---|
| II Sam. 13:11-13 | He [Amnon] caught hold of her [Tamar] and said to her, "Come lie with me, sister." But she said to him, "Don't, brother. Don't force me... please, speak to the king; he will not refuse me to you.[148] |

### Description of Violation

The Torah forbids sexual relations between brother and sister, even if they share only one parent. How then does Tamar declare that David would not refuse her to her half-brother? Would David indeed violate this Torah law?

---

147. See also Lev. 20:17 and Deut. 27:22. These verses stress that sexual relations are forbidden between brother and sister even if they share only one parent.
148. Amnon was the son of Ahinoam (II Sam. 3:2), and Tamar was the daughter of Maacah the Geshurite (ibid. 3:3; 13:1). Thus Amnon and Tamar shared the same father, David, but were not of the same mother.

| Rabbinic Resolution | |
|---|---|
| **BT _Sanhedrin_ 21a** | תמר בת יפת תואר היתה שנאמר דבר נא באזני המלך כי לא ימנעני ממך (ש"ב יג:יג) ואי סלקא דעתך בת נישואין הואי אחתיה מי הוה שריא ליה? אלא שמע מינה בת יפת תואר היתה |
| | Tamar was the daughter of a _yefat toar_,[149] as it is written, "Please, speak to the king; he will not refuse me to you" (II Sam. 13:13). If she was the offspring of a legitimate marriage, how could his sister have been granted him in marriage? We must therefore infer that she was the daughter of a _yefat toar_. |

### Analysis of Rabbinic Resolution

Our source indicates that Tamar was the daughter of a woman taken captive in war,[150] and thus, in terms of the law of incest, was not related to any of David's children.[151] Therefore, Amnon was indeed permitted to marry her, and the violation is denied.[152]

---

149. A _yefat toar_ is a captive woman taken as a concubine because of her beauty (Deut. 21:10-13). Maacah was probably taken captive in the war David fought against Geshur (I Sam. 27:8).

150. Cf. BT _Yevamot_ 22a, BT _Kiddushin_ 22a. See also Rambam, _Hilkhot Melakhim_ 6:8.

151. See Tosafot, _Sanhedrin_ 21a, s.v. _de-iy_.

152. If Tamar was permitted to Amnon, one wonders why he underwent elaborate plans to rape her when he could have simply married her. For an attempt to resolve this issue in the light of rabbinic literature, see S. Bar Efrat's _Ha-Itzuv ha-Omanuti be-Sippur ha-Mikra_ [Hebrew] (Jerusalem, 1979), p. 199. Cf. Abravanel, II Sam. 13:13, who assumes that Tamar was not permitted to Amnon, and that her suggestion was a stall tactic.

# Chapter 33
## Violation Relating to the Law of Murder

| Torah | |
|---|---|
| Num. 35:30-33 | If anyone kills a person, the manslayer may be executed only on the evidence of witnesses; the testimony of a single witness against a person shall not suffice for a sentence of death. You may not accept a ransom for the life of a murderer who is guilty of a capital crime; he must be put to death. Nor may you accept ransom in lieu of flight to a city of refuge, enabling one to return to live on his land before the death of the Kohen. You shall not pollute the land in which you live; for blood pollutes the land, and the land can have no expiration for blood that is shed on it, except by the blood of him who shed it. |

| Prophets | |
|---|---|
| II Sam. 14:4, 6-7; 11 | The woman of Tekoa said... "your maidservant had two sons. The two of them came to blows out in the fields where there was no one to stop them, and one of them struck the other and killed him. Then the whole clan confronted your maidservant and said, hand over the one who killed his brother, that we may put him to death for the slaying of his brother...." The king said to the woman, "Go home. I will issue and order on your behalf... as the Lord, God lives, not a hair of your son shall fall to the ground." |

## Description of Violation

The Torah requires life for a life. Since murder is a capital offense, how did David issue an order releasing the murderer in II Sam. 14 from the death penalty? In addition, escape to a city of refuge seems not to be an option. And if the homicide was committed without intent, David seems to be ignorant of the laws of the city of refuge.

| Rabbinic Resolution | |
|---|---|
| **Targum Jonathan II Sam. 14:11** | ידכר כען מלכא מה דכתיב בספר אוריתא דה' א-להיך בדיל לאסגאה אורחא קדם גאל דמא לחבלא.<br><br>May the king now remember that which is written in the book of Law of the Lord your God that the way should be made long before the avenger of the blood who is out to destroy. |

## Analysis of Rabbinic Resolution

According to Jonathan's translation, the woman of Tekoa reminded David of the laws of the unintentional murderer. This implies that her son killed without intention.[153] Thus, David upheld the law by protecting him,[154] and no violation occurred.

---

153. The intentional murderer is not protected in the way Jonathan describes (see Exod. 21:14, Num. 35:20-21, Deut. 19:6).
154. Intentional murder is not protected by escape to a city of refuge. This rendition of Jonathan implies that the murder was not committed with intent. Ralbag explains that even if the murder was committed intentionally, David did not violate Torah law in his ruling. The Torah only allows the execution of the death penalty if the crime was witnessed by two people (Deut. 17:6). In the woman's account of the story, there is no mention of witnesses. Assuming David thought this was the case, he did not violate Torah law in his ruling. Ralbag also explains that David based his ruling on his special rights as king. Even if David thought the crime was witnessed by two people, and *was* intentional, he could save the boy by exercising those special rights. Thus, according to this answer, a king is not only permitted to be stringent in his rulings because of his special rights, but he may be lenient as well.

# Chapter 34

# Violation of the Law Against Vicarious Punishment

| Torah | |
|---|---|
| **Deut. 24:16** | Parents shall not be put to death for children, or children be put to death for parents. A person shall be put to death only for his own crime. |

| Prophets | |
|---|---|
| **II Sam. 21:5-6** | The Gibeonites answered him... The man who massacred us and planned to exterminate us, so that we should not survive in all the territory of Israel,[155] let seven of his male issue be handed over to us, and we will impale them...and the king replied, "I will do so." |

### Description of Violation

The Torah prohibits vicarious punishment.[156] We find, however, that David allows seven descendants of Saul to be put to death for sins committed by Saul himself (II Sam. 21:5-6). Thus vicarious punishment seems to be tolerated.

---

155. Such an act of Saul's against the Gibeonites is not recorded in the Bible. See JT *Sanhedrin* 6:7, JT *Kiddushin* 4:1, BT *Yevamot* 78b, *Bemidbar Rabbah* 8:4, for an aggadic account of Saul's sin to the Gibeonites.

156. Deut. 24:16 does not allow children to be punished for sins committed by their parents. The Torah also says, however, "He does not remit all punishment, but visits the iniquity of fathers upon children" (Exod. 34:7). David, however, is in violation of Deut. 24:16 for doing so. See *Midrash Tannaim Deut.* 24:16. See also, above, ch. 3.

| Rabbinic Resolutions | |
|---|---|
| **BT *Yevamot* 79a** | ויקרא המלך לגבעונים ויאמר אליהם מה אעשה לכם.... ויאמרו לו הגבעונים... יותן לנו שבעה אנשים מבניו והוקענום וגו' מיפייס ולא פייייסינהו. ויקח המלך את שני בני רצפה בת איה אשר ילדה לשאול... ואת חמשת בני מיכל... והא כתיב (דב' כד:טז) לא יומתו אבות על בנים ובנים לא יומתו על אבות... מוטב שתיעקר אות אחת מן התורה ואל יתחלל שם שמים בפרהסיא.<br><br>The king summoned the Gibeonites and spoke to them, "What shall I do for you? ... The Gibeonites answered him.... Let seven of his [Saul's] male issue be handed over to us and we will impale them. He tried to pacify them to no avail. The king took the two sons that Rizpah daughter of Aiah... bore to Saul... and the five sons of Michal...." But surely it is written, "Parents shall not be put to death for children or children be put to death for parents" (Deut. 24:16)....[157] It is better that a letter be rooted out of the Torah than the Divine name shall be publicly profaned.[158] |
| ***Bemidbar Rabbah* 8:4** | מיד שלח דוד וקרא להם: מה לכם ולבית שאול? על שפסק את מזונינו ועל שהמית ממנו שבעה אנשים<br><br>David sent them [Gibeonites], and called to them, "What matter do you have to settle with the house of Saul?" [They answered] the house of Saul put a cease to our food and killed seven of our people. |

---

157. The passage in *Bemidbar Rabbah* 8:4 reads here: "And yet these children died for the sins of their father!"

158. God's name would have been profaned had the crime against the Gibeonites been allowed to go unpunished. The letter uprooted here is the violation of Deut. 24:16.

## Analysis of Rabbinic Resolution

BT *Yevamot* 79a is a classic example of *horaʾat shaʾah*. David's responsibility was to put an end to the famine and he thus consented to the demands of the Gibeonites even though they violated Torah law.[159]

*Bemidbar Rabbah* 8:4 indicates that these seven people deserved to die for the role they allegedly played in the killing of the Gibeonites. Thus David did not kill innocent men and the violation is denied.

---

159. See Malbim's explanation (II Sam. 21:6) of Rambam, *Hilkhot Melakhim* 3:10, regarding justification for David's actions in this case.

# Chapter 35

## Violation in not Burying the Dead

| Torah | |
|---|---|
| **Deut. 21:22-23** | If a man is guilty of a capital offense and is put to death and you impale him on a stake, you must not let his corpse remain on the stake overnight, but must bury him the same day. For an impaled body is an affront to God[160]; you shall not defile the land that the Lord your God is giving you to possess. |

| Prophets | |
|---|---|
| **II Sam. 21:9-10** | They impaled them on the mountain before the Lord... they were put to death in the first days of the harvest, the beginning of the barley harvest. Then Rizpah... stayed there from the beginning of the harvest until rain from the sky fell on them; she did not let the birds of the sky settle on them by day or the wild beast by night. |

---

160. The Talmud explains that if a body is allowed to hang overnight, people will be reminded that someone sinned against God (BT *Sanhedrin* 46a). Therefore, an impaled body is an affront to God.

## Description of Violation

The Torah commands the immediate burial of a person who was hanged. The plain meaning of the text is that the seven bodies were hanging for a very long time.[161] Yet no mention is made of this violation.[162]

| Rabbinic Resolutions | |
|---|---|
| JT *Kiddushin* 4:1 | מה חטאו אילו שנישתנית עליהן מדת הדין? על שפשטו ידיהן בגרים גרורים. אמרו מה אם אלו שלא נתגיירו לשם שמים ראו היאך תבע הקב"ה את דמו, המתגייר לשם שמים על אחת כמה וכמה. אין א-לוה כא-להיהן ואין אומה כאומתכם ואין לנו להידבק אלא בכם. הרבה גרים נתגיירו באותה שעה. |
| | What was, their sin that their punishment should be changed so?[163] Because they attacked the converts. The nations would say, "If this is how God stands behind those who did not convert for spiritual purposes,[164] how much more so will He stand behind those who do convert for spiritual purposes. There is no God like theirs and no nation like theirs, and we should cleave to them." At that moment many people converted to become Israelites. |

---

161. Rashi supports this reading (II Sam. 21:10). Abravanel maintains that rain miraculously fell in the days of the barley harvest. He nevertheless agrees that the bodies were left hanging long enough to be in violation of Torah law.
162. Joshua took care with this regard even in the burial of the foreign kings of Canaan (see Josh. 8:29, 10:27).
163. Why did they deserve to have their bodies hang from a tree for so long against Torah law?
164. The Gibeonites did not convert for spiritual purposes, but to save their lives from the powerful Israelite army. Cf. Joshua 9.

| BT *Yevamot* 79a | ותקח רצפה... מתחלת קציר עד נתך מים עליהם מן השמים. ולא נתנה עוף השמים לנוח עליהם יומם וחית השדה לילה (ש"ב כא:י) והכתיב לא תלין נבלתו על העץ (דב' כא:כג) מוטב שתיעקר אות אחת מן התורה ויתקדש שם שמים בפרהסיא שהיו עוברים ושבים ואומרים, מה טיבן של אלו? הללו בני מלכים הם. ומה עשו? פשטו ידיהם בגרים גרורים. אמרו אין לך אומה שראויה להדבק בו כזו. ומה בני מלכים כך, בני הדיוטות על אחת כמה וכמה! והגרים גרורים כך. ישראל על אחת כמה וכמה! מיד נתוספו על ישראל מאה וחמישים אלף. |
| --- | --- |

Then Rizpah... stayed there from the beginning of the harvest until rain from the sky fell on them; she did not let the birds of the sky settle on them by day or the wild beast by night (II Sam. 21:10). But surely it is written, "His body shall not remain all night upon the tree" (Deut. 21:23) It is proper that a letter be rooted out of the Torah,[165] so that thereby the heavenly name shall be publicly hallowed. For passers-by were inquiring, "What kind of men are these?" These are princes. "And what have they done?" They laid their hands on forced converts. Then they said: There is no nation which one ought to join as much as this one. If the punishment of princes was so great, how much more, that of common people! And if such was the justice done for forced converts, how much more so for Israelites.[166] Immediately 150,000 converts joined the ranks of Israel.

165. God's name is hallowed by the severe punishment for the unfair treatment of converts. The letter that is uprooted here, is the violation of Deut. 21:22-23.
166. In other words, how much more so would God stand behind true converts who, subsequent to their conversion would be considered Israelites.

## Analysis of Rabbinic Resolutions

JT *Kiddushin* 4:1 and BT *Yevamot* 79a are classical example of *hora'ot sha'ah*. BT *Yevamot* 79a teaches that Torah law may be violated in order to preserve the sanctity and honor of God's name.[167] In this case it was the severe punishment for the unfair treatment of converts that sanctified God's name. Thus the violation is explained away as a *hora'at sha'ah*.

---

167. BT *Berakhot* 54a teaches this from *et la-asot la-YHVH hefeiru Toratekha* (Ps. 119:126). Rashi explains that one may violate the Torah to perform God's immediate bidding. After all, the Deity is God, not the Torah, which is the point that Ps. 119:126 makes.

# Chapter 36
# Violation of the Law Against Vicarious Punishment

| Torah | |
|---|---|
| Deut. 24:16 | A person shall be put to death only for his own crime. |

| Prophets | |
|---|---|
| II Sam. 24:15-17 | The Lord sent a pestilence upon Israel from morning until the set time and 70,000 [168] people died, from Dan to Beersheba. When David saw the angel striking down the people, he said to the Lord, "I alone am guilty, I alone have done wrong; but these poor sheep, what have they done? Let Your hand fall upon me and my father's house." |

### Description of Violation

The Torah prohibits vicarious punishment. We find, however, in II Sam. 24:15-17 that 70,000 people die as a consequence of David's sin. Thus vicarious punishment seems to be tolerated.

---

168. According to BT *Berakhot* 62b, Avishai ben Zeruiah alone died. However, whether 70,000 died or if only one person died as a consequence of David's sin, it seems vicarious punishment is tolerated.

| Rabbinic Resolutions | |
|---|---|
| *Midrash* <br> *Tehillim* 17:4 | כל אותן אלפים שנפלו במלחמה בימי דוד לא נפלו אלא על שלא תבעו בנין בית המקדש <br><br> All the thousands who died in war[169] in the days of David, died because they did not demand the building of the Temple. |

*Midrash Tehillim* 17:4 explains that the 70,000 people did not die as a consequence of David's sins, but because of their negligence with regards to the building of the Temple.[170] Thus the violation is denied.

The following passage does not specifically address this issue but can, by analogy, serve as a resolution.

| *Midrash* <br> *Tannaim,* <br> Deut. 24:16 | לא יומתו אבות על בנים (דב' כד:טז) לפי שהוא אומר פקד עון אבות על בנים (שמ' כ:ה) שומע אני אף מחוייבי מיתת בית דין, ת"ל לא יומתו אבות על בנים. <br><br> "Parents shall not be put to death for children" (Deut. 24:16), since Scripture states, "visiting the guilt of fathers upon their children" (Exod. 20:5). I might have thought that such is the case even pertaining to those of capital crimes.[171] Therefore, Scripture states, "Parents shall not be put to death for children." |

---

169. *Midrash Tehillim* 17:4 reads, "All the thousands who died in war." However, based on the previous passage in the Midrash, the 70,000 people who died in II Sam. 24 are included.
170. See above, Chapter 6. Negligence in building the Temple is not a capital offense. Perhaps this is given as the reason for the death of the 70,000 because God commands David to buy the land where the Temple would be built to end the pestilence. See Radak, II Sam. 24:25.
171. That a child can be put to death by the courts for a capital crime committed by his father. This cannot be done. But God can visit the guilt of one party to another.

*Midrash Tannaim*, Deut. 24:16, indicates that the human courts have no right to punish one person for the sins of another. However, the heavenly court does punish one for the sins of another, as indicated by Exod. 20:5. The 70,000 people who died as a consequence of David's sin were not put to death by the earthly court. Thus no vicarious punishment was imposed by a human court and the violation is explained away.[172]

---

172. For a rabbinic discussion on the different applications of Exod. 20:5 and Deut. 24:16, see Manasseh ben Israel's *Conciliator*, vol.1, #104, pp. 164-167.

# Chapters 37-41
## *Hora'at Sha'ah* by Divine Decree

## Chapter 37: Reasons for Killing Achan

| Torah | |
|---|---|
| Exod. 23:7 | Do not bring death on the innocent. |

| Prophets | |
|---|---|
| Josh. 7:20-26 | Achan answered Joshua, "It is true, I have sinned against the God of Israel. This is what I did: I saw among the spoil a fine Shinar mantle.... They are buried in the ground in my tent.... Then Joshua, and all Israel with him, took Achan, ... and all Israel pelted him with stones. |

### Description of Violation

There is no precedent in the Torah for Joshua killing Achan for his crime. Surely he is not deserving of the death penalty. Taking from the proscribed spoils of Jericho can be no worse than taking from the spoils of the *ir ha-niddahat*,[173] the punishment of which is not the death penalty.

---

173. Deut. 13:13-19; v.18: "Let nothing that has been doomed stick to your hands."

| Rabbinic Resolutions | |
|---|---|
| *Tanhuma,* **Vayyeshev** [174] | תדע לך כח החרם... וכן אתה מוציא בעכן נאמר, הלא עכן בן זרח מעל מעל בחרם ועל כל עדת ישראל היה קצף (יהושע כב:ב) <br><br> We learn the severity of a ban... also from Achan, regarding where it says, "When Achan son of Zerah violated the ban, anger struck the whole community of Israel." |

**Analysis of Rabbinic Resolution**

This source explains the severity of a ban, showing the losses Israel suffered as a result of its violation. Joshua wanted to eradicate the sin from Israel, and thus acted accordingly to calm God's anger over Israel.[175] Ultimately, however, it is God's command to Joshua, that justifies Joshua's action, for God Himself ordered the execution of Achan (Joshua 7:15). Therefore this violation is denied and categorized as *hora'at sha'ah* by Divine decree.

---

174. This passage can also be found in *Pirkei de-Rabbi Eliezer* 38.
175. See Rambam, *Hilkhot Sanhedrin* 18:6, where Joshua's actions are described either as *hora'at sha'ah*, or that his actions were based on his special legal right as king, to kill someone who breaks his precepts. Joshua saw a threat to Israel in Achan's actions, and as leader acted accordingly. See also Rambam, *Hilkhot Rotze'ah* 2:4, *Hilkhot Melakhim* 3:10; Ramban, Lev. 27-29; Rashba, *Nedarim* 7a.

# Chapter 38
## Violations Regarding Sacrifice

| Torah | |
|---|---|
| **Num. 18:4** | They [Levites] shall be attached to you [priest] and discharge the duties of the Tent of Meeting, all the services of the Tent, but no outsider shall intrude upon you. |
| **Deut. 12:2-3** | You must destroy all the sites at which the nations you are to dispossess worshipped their gods, whether on lofty mountains and on hills or under any luxuriant tree. Tear down their altars, smash their pillars, burn their Asherim, and cut down the images of their gods, obliterating their name from that site. |

| Prophets | |
|---|---|
| **Judg. 6:25-26** | That night the Lord said to him, "Take the bull belonging to your father and another bull seven years old; pull down the altar of Baal which belongs to your father, and cut down the Asherah which is beside it. Then build an altar to the Lord your God, on the level ground on top of this stronghold. Take the other bull and offer it as a burnt offering using the wood of Asherah that you have cut down." So Gideon took ten of his servants and did as the Lord had told him; but as he was afraid to do it by day he did it by night. |

## Description of Violation

Torah law forbids the offering of sacrifices outside the Tent of Meeting. In addition, an outsider, one not of the sons of Aaron,[176] is forbidden to offer sacrifices even inside the Tent of Meeting. The Torah also calls for the uprooting and burning of Asherim. Gideon, a Manassite (Judg. 6:15), by the word of God, offers a sacrifice outside the precincts of the Tent of meeting, and uses the Asherah as firewood. There seems to be wide-spread ignorance of Torah Law regarding sacrifice.[177]

| Rabbinic Resolution | |
|---|---|
| BT *Temurah* 28b [178] | שמונה דברים התירו באותו לילה: חוץ, לילה, וזרות, וכלי שרת, וכלי שרת, וכלי אשרה, ועצי אשרה ומוקצה, ונעבד |
| | Eight things were permitted that night: (1) an offering brought outside the Tabernacle, (2) offering brought at night, (3) the officiating by a non-priest, (4) without a ministering vessel, (5) the ministering with vessels of Ashereh, (6) using the wood of Asherah, (7) *muktzeh* and (8) *ne'evad*.[179] |

---

176. "So that no outsider, one not of Aaron's offspring should presume to offer incense before the Lord" (Num. 17:5).

177. In rabbinic literature ten transgressions are found in Gideon's actions. See BT *Temurah* 28b-29a, JT *Megillah* 1:12, *Bemidbar Rabbah*, Naso 14:1. Listed are actions which transgress the simple meaning of the text. For instance, the Rabbis list as a violation Gideon's offering taking place at night. This violation is not included here because the rabbinic derivation of this ruling, BT *Zevahim* 98a, does not reflect the simple meaning of the verse (Lev. 7:38).

178. The parallel passage in JT *Megillah* lists seven transgressions, omitting both transgressions involving ministering vessels, and adding the transgression of making an altar from stones unfit for use. *Bemidbar Rabbah*, Naso 14:1, mentions a single transgression of the son of an idolater offering a sacrifice. The three transgressions listed here are mentioned both in BT *Temurah* and JT *Megillah*.

179. *Muktzeh* and *ne'evad* are explained in BT *Terumah* 28a.

## Analysis of Rabbinic Resolution

The Rabbis acknowledged that these actions of Gideon violated Torah law. However, they are justified as acts of *hora'at sha'ah*.[180]

---

180. Reasons why Gideon was commanded to violate these laws are offered by Ralbag and Abravanel, Judg. 6:26.

# Chapter 39
## Violation of Proper Military Procedure

| | Torah |
|---|---|
| | **Torah** |
| **Deut. 20:1, 5-8** | When you take the field against your enemies... then the officials shall address the troops, as follows, "Is there anyone who has built a new house but has not dedicated it? Let him go back to his home lest he die in battle and another dedicate it. Is there anyone who has planted a vineyard but has not harvested it? Let him go back to his home, lest he die in battle and another initiate it. Is there anyone who has paid the bride-price for a wife but who has not yet married her? Let him go back to his home lest he die in battle and another marry." The officials shall go on addressing the troops and say, "Is there anyone afraid and disheartened? Let him go back to his home lest the courage of his comrades flag like his." |
| **Deut. 24:5** | When a man has taken a bride, he shall not go out with the army or be assigned to it for any purpose; he shall be exempt one year for the sake of his household, to give happiness to the woman he married. |

| Prophets | |
| --- | --- |
| Judg. 7:2-3, 5, 7 | The Lord said to Gideon, "You have too many troops with you.... Therefore announce to the men, Let anybody who is timid and fearful turn back...." The Lord said to Gideon, "There are still too many troops. Take them down to the water.... Set apart those who lap up the water with their tongues like dogs, from all those who get down on their knees to drink." Then the Lord said to Gideon, "I will deliver you and I will put Midian into your hands through the three hundred lappers. Let the rest of the troops go home." |

### Description of Violation

The Torah exempts certain people from joining in the war effort. In comparison of the Torah's and Gideon's exemptions by the word of God, two problems exist. First, Gideon should not have specifically been told by God to allow the timid to turn back. The Torah commands that this always be done. This obscure method seems to be ignorant of the Torah's military protocol.

| Rabbinic Resolutions | |
| --- | --- |
| BT *Sotah* 44b | במה דברים אמורים? במלחמת הרשות, אבל במלחמת מצוה הכל יוצאין, אפילו חתן מחדרו וכלה מחופתה. |
| | To what does all the foregoing apply?[181] To voluntary wars,[182] but in obligatory wars[183] all go forth, even a bridegroom from his chamber and a bride from her canopy. |

181. "Foregoing" refers to commandments in Deut. 20:1, 5-8, and Deut. 24:5.
182. Voluntary wars are those fought to increase the borders of Israel, or for a king to show his might or gain more subjects.
183. Obligatory wars include the conquest of Canaan, the annihilation of Amalek, and wars fought in defense of Israel.

| *Tanhuma,* **Toledot 19** [184] | והיה שארית יעקב (מיכה ה:ו) זה היה השארית שאמר הקב"ה לאליהו והשארית בישראל שבעת אלפים. כל הברכים וגו' (מ"א יט:יח) ואלו הן שהפריש בימי גדעון שנ' כל אשר ילך בלשונו מן המים (שופ' ז:ה) וכל יתר העם כרעו על ברכיהם לשתות מים שם שהיו משתחווים לע"ז. ומאלו שלש מאות שלא כרעו ולא השתחוו לעבודה זרה עמדו אלה ז' אלפים. |
|---|---|
| | "The remnant of Jacob shall be..." (Micah 5:6). God spoke of this remnant to Elijah, "I will leave in Israel only seven thousand. Every knee that has not knelt to Baal..." (I Kings 19:18). These were the ones who were separated in the days of Gideon, as it says, "All those who lap up the water with their tongues" (Judg. 7:5). The rest of the nation knelt on their knees to drink water there, for they bowed to [worshipped] false gods. And from these three hundred who did not kneel and did not bow to false gods were descended these seven thousand. |

### Analysis of Rabbinic Resolution

BT *Sotah* 44a indicates that these exemptions were made only prior to voluntary wars. However, before obligatory wars, such exemptions were not made. All people, without exception, participate in the war effort. Since Gideon's war was one of self-defense of Israel,[185] no exemptions were permitted. This explains why it was necessary for Gideon to be told to send home those who were afraid. Thus, God's declaration to Gideon does not imply ignorance of military procedure on the part of the latter. *Tanhuma, Toledot*, explains why the specific method mentioned in the text was used in sending people home. It was God's way of dismissing idol worshippers, thus preventing them from hampering the war effort. Gideon's actions can be classified as *hora'at sha'ah* by Divine decree.

---

184. See also *Bereshit Rabbati*, p. 110.
185. The war was also fought against Amalek; see Judg. 6:33.

# Chapter 40
# Violations Regarding Nazirite Laws

| Torah | |
|---|---|
| **Num. 6:3-6** | He [the Nazir] shall abstain from wine and any other intoxicant; he shall not drink vinegar or wine or any other intoxicant, neither shall he drink anything in which grapes have been steeped, nor eat grapes fresh or dried. Throughout his term as Nazir he may not eat anything that is obtained from the grapevine, even seeds or skin. Throughout the term of his vow as Nazir, no razor shall touch his head. Throughout the term that he has set apart for the Lord, he shall not go in where there is a dead person. |

| Prophets | |
|---|---|
| **Judg. 13:3-5** | An angel of the Lord appeared to the woman and said to her, "You are barren and have borne no children, but you shall conceive and bear a son. Now be careful not to drink wine or other intoxicant or eat anything unclean. For you are going to conceive and bear a son. Let no razor touch his head, for the boy is to be a Nazir to God from the womb on." |

**Description of Violation**

The Torah lists three rules of the Nazir: (1) He may not eat or drink anything from the vine, (2) a razor cannot touch his hair, (3) he may not come into contact with a dead body.

The Nazir himself is only warned regarding the second rule. Furthermore, the Nazir's mother, not the Nazir, is warned about the first rule. Finally, the third rule is not mentioned at all! Such unawareness of simple Torah law must be explained.

| Rabbinic Resolutions | |
|---|---|
| BT *Nazir* 4a | מה בין נזיר עולם לנזיר שמשון? נזיר עולם, הכביד שערו מיקל בתער ומביא שלש בהמות ואם נטמא מביא קרבן טומאה. נזיר שמשון הכביד שערו אינו מיקל ואם נטמא אינו מביא קרבן טומאה.<br><br>What difference is there between a Nazir like Samson and a life-Nazir? A life-Nazir, if his hair becomes heavy, may thin it with a razor and offer three animal sacrifices, while, if he becomes ritually defiled, he must offer the sacrifice prescribed for defilement. The Nazir like Samson is not permitted to thin his hair should it become heavy, and if ritually defiled does not offer the prescribed sacrifice. |
| *Bemidbar Rabbah* 10:5 (#1) | גלוי היה לפני הקב"ה ששמשון יהיה הולך אחר עיניו. לפיכך הזהירו בנזיר שלא יהיה שותה יין, לפי שהיין מביא לידי זימה.<br><br>It was clear to God that Samson would follow his desires. Therefore, God warned him with the prohibitions of a Nazir so that he should not drink wine because wine leads to depravity. |
| *Bemidbar Rabbah* 10:5 (#2) | ואל תאכלי כל טמא. ואין טמא אלא איסור שהתורה הזהירה לנזיר שלא לאכול כלום מכל אשר יוצא מגפן היין.<br><br>Do not eat anything unclean, and "unclean" describes forbidden foods the Torah warns a Nazir not to eat from, mainly anything coming from the grapevine. |

| | |
|---|---|
| **Bemidbar Rabbah 10:5** (#3) | מהו שאמר "מן הבטן"? (שופ' יג:ה) לקיים מה שנאמר בטרם אצרך בבטן ידעתיך (ירמ' א:ה).<br><br>What is meant by, "the boy is to be a Nazir to God from the womb on"? To fulfill what is said, "before I created you in the womb, I selected you" (Jer. 1:5). |
| **BT Nazir 4b** (#1) | נזיר שמשון מותר ליטמא למתים שכן מצינו בשמשון שניטמא.<br><br>A Nazir such as Samson is permitted to defile himself deliberately by contact with the dead, for Samson himself did so. |
| **BT Nazir 4b** (#2) | ושמשון לאו נזיר היה? והכתיב נזיר א-להים יהיה נער מן הבטן (שופ' יג:ה) התם מלאך הוא דקאמר.<br><br>But was not Samson a Nazir in the ordinary sense? Surely the verse states, "For the child shall be a Nazir unto God from the womb" (Judg. 13:5). It was the angel who said this. |

## Analysis of Rabbinic Resolution

BT *Nazir* 4a implies that Samson was commanded to refrain from anything coming from the grapevine and any intoxicant, just like his mother, and just like any Nazir. *Bemidbar Rabbah* 10:5 (#1) as well takes this for granted. It would seem, then, that Samson's mother was told to avoid all food and drink forbidden to a Nazir as *Bemidbar Rabbah* 10:5 (#2) indicates, in order to prepare her son for this command. *Bemidbar Rabbah* 10:5 (#3) seems to indicate that forbidden foods to a Nazir applied to Samson in the womb.[186] Surely then, they applied to him after he was born. This is why the ruling that Samson avoid what comes from the grapevine is not told to his mother explicitly in the text, for it is obvious.

---

186. See Ralbag, Judg. 13:3, who explains that whatever a woman eats or drinks is passed into the womb. Since Samson was a "Nazir from the womb," his mother was told to avoid eating anything from the vine and intoxicating drink for her entire pregnancy, so as not to pass these forbidden foods to him."

Regarding the law of death defilement, BT *Nazir* 4b (#1) indicates that such a law never pertained to Samson at all. BT *Nazir* 4b (#2) states this and qualifies it. Because an angel commanded Samson's Nazirship, he was considered such only with regards to what the angel said. The laws that the angel mentioned were incumbent on Samson, and that which the angel did not mention was not incumbent on Samson.[187] Therefore, no violation is acknowledged and the resolution is categorized as *hora'at sha'ah* by Divine decree.

---

187. See Rashi, Nazir 4b, s.v. *malakh hu de-ka'amar*. Tosafot, ibid., s.v. *hatam*. Rambam, *Hilkhot Nezirut* 3:13, and Radbaz, ad. loc.

# Chapter 41
# Violation Relating to Lying

| Torah | |
|---|---|
| Exod. 23:7 | Keep far from a false charge.[188] |

| Prophets | |
|---|---|
| I Sam. 16:2 | Samuel replied, "How can I go? If Saul hears it, he will kill me." The Lord answered, "Take a heifer with you and say, I have come to sacrifice to the Lord...." |

## Description of Violation

Samuel's purpose in going to Bethlehem was to crown David king. Why is he commanded to hide this intention behind a stated false pretense?[189]

---

188. The command is understood here, simply as a prohibition against lying. That the rabbis understand the verse in this way is apparent from BT *Ketuvot* 17a. (Rambam omits this prohibition in his list of commandments, and understands the verse to prohibit false testimony. See *Hilkhot To'en ve-Nit'an* 16:10, *Hilkhot Sanhedrin* 21:7.)

189. BT *Pesahim* 8b explains that God did not tell Samuel that Saul simply would not harm him because when danger is probable (as in the case of Samuel crowning David while Saul was yet king), one cannot rely totally on intervention from God. Another defense was necessary and this was Samuel's fabrication. See Abravanel, I Sam. 16:2.

| Rabbinic Resolution | |
|---|---|
| BT *Yevamot* 65b | מצוה (לשנות מפני השלום) שנאמר ויאמר שמואל איך אלך ושמע שאול והרגני. ויאמר ה' עגלת בקר תקח בידך ואמרת לזבח לה' באתי (ש"א טז:ב).<br><br>It is a commandment to modify a statement in the interests of maintaining peace for it is stated (I Sam 16:2): Samuel replied, "How can I go? If Saul hears of it, he will kill me." The Lord answered, "Take a heifer with you and say, I have come to sacrifice to the Lord." |

**Analysis of Rabbinic Resolution**

This source is a classical case of *hora'at sha'ah*. God's command to violate a Torah law is warranted by the situation at hand. Samuel is afraid for his life and acts accordingly under the instruction of God.[190] Thus, the violation is explained away,[191] under the category of *hora'at sha'ah* by Divine decree.

---

190. Post-rabbinic commentaries explain that, even though the Talmud states Samuel lied, the plain meaning of the text does not necessarily imply that Samuel openly did so. See Maharsha, *Yevamot* 65b. See also, Radak, I Sam. 16:2, who explains that Samuel was being told to draw attention to what he was doing as a sign of assurance that no harm would come to him. This in line with God's response to Moses' fear of being starved to death by thirsty Israelites at Exod. 17:4. God told Moses to pass right before the people in the next verse, as if to assure him that he would come to no harm. Samuel, according to Radak, is similarly assured here. No harm can come to someone who heeds the word of God!
191. There are other instances of lying in the books of Joshua, Judges, and Samuel which are neither acknowledged or resolved by the Rabbis. The resolution offered here can, by analogy, resolve some of those instances of lying as well. See I Sam. 19:14, ibid. 20:28-29.

# Analyses and Conclusions

Six Categories of Violations

In the previous chapters the violations have been categorized according to their resolutions. However other categorizations can be introduced relating to the type of violation and to the perpetrator of the violation. Herewith we introduce a new set of categories, whose purpose is to determine if the Rabbis treated certain types of violations or certain violators according to a fixed pattern. Conclusions will be drawn from the evidence examined in the previous chapters and here. The following is a list of the classifications of the violations:

1. Violations of Positive Commandments[192]

   Most violations treated in this study involve a person *doing* something which he should not have done. Category 1 lists violations where a person failed to do something he should have done. An example of this is Samson's disregard of the ritual prescribed concerning a Nazir who contacted defilement from a dead body (see ch. 12).

2. Violations Intended Which Were Never Actually Committed

   Category 2 includes intended actions which, if carried out, would have violated the Torah. An example is David's pronouncement of the death penalty for the sheep-stealer in Nathan's parable (II Sam. 12:4-6). The execution of David's ruling would have violated the Torah. Of course the sheep-stealer does not exist and David's ruling was never carried

---

192. The remaining categories consist of violations of negative commandments and are broken down accordingly.

out (see ch. 31). This category also includes the contrived story in which David rules that an alleged murderer be allowed to go free (see ch. 33).

3. Violation of Laws Regarding Sacrifice

Category 3 includes many examples, most of them gathered together in chapter 8. Violations range from non-priests offering sacrifice to sacrifice outside the precincts of the Tent of Meeting, to offering female cows as burnt offerings (see also ch. 16).

4. Violations Concerning the Unlawful Taking of a Life

Category 4 includes apparent violations relating to the law of murder, as well as the following cases: The suicides of Samson, Saul, Saul's armor bearer and Ahithophel[193] (ch. 13); violations relating to vicarious punishment (chs. 3, 5, 34, 36); overly stringent judicial decisions (chs. 20, 24, 27, 31, 37); court proceedings required by the Torah which were deficient, yet the death penalty was pronounced (ch. 4, 21, 28); a deserving death penalty was not enforced (ch. 33).

5. Violations of Laws Pertaining to Idolatry and the Laws Governing Relations with Non-Israelites

Category 5 includes apparent violations regarding worship of anything besides the God of Israel. Perpetrators in this section include such righteous figures as Joshua (ch. 1) and David (ch. 23). Two apparent violations are also recorded in this section regarding relations with the seven nations of Canaan (ch. 2) and Ammon (ch. 30).

6. Violations of Ritual Law

The following violations of ritual law are included: *kashrut* laws (ch. 11), priestly laws (ch. 15, 29), law relating to divination, (ch. 19), burial

---

193. Abimelech's request of his lad to kill him is not dealt with in this study, as explained in ch. 13, note 66.

laws (ch. 26, 35); law relating to the marriage relationship (ch. 22, 25); Nazirite laws (ch. 12, 40). The following is a listing of all violations (by chapter) according to the six categories introduced above:[194]

a. Violations of Positive Commandments: 2, 6, 7, 9, 12, 17, 18, 33, 35, 39.

b. Intended Violations Which Were Never Actually Committed: 20, 24, 31, 32, 33, 41.

c. Violations of Laws Regarding Sacrifice: 8, 16, 38.

d. Violations Concerning the Unlawful Taking of a Life: 3, 4, 5, 10, 13, 20, 21, 24, 27, 28, 31, 33, 34, 36, 37.

e. Violations of Laws Pertaining to Idolatry and the Laws Governing Relations with Non-Israelites: 1, 2, 14, 22, 23, 30.

f. Violations of Ritual Laws: 11, 12, 15, 19, 25, 26, 29, 35, 40.

Resolutions

The first three categories of resolutions listed in this study (Violation Denied; Violation Explained Away; Hora'at Sha'ah) account for the biblical narrator's apparent unawareness of violation by postulating that, in effect, no violation has occurred. The fourth category acknowledges violation and often suggests that the biblical author really acknowledged the violation as well. The fifth category recognizes the violation but excuses it. This study reveals that of the 63 passages mentioned here which resolve violations unnoticed by the biblical narrator, 55 stem from rabbinic literature prior to and including the era of the Babylonian Talmud. In contrast, regarding the seven passages mentioned here which acknowledge a violation, only three stem from classical rabbinic literature. Thus, it seems to be the trend of later (post-Babylonian Talmud) rabbinic literature to acknowledge sin. There are two examples in this study where a violation denied or

---

194. Some of these violations may be included in two or more categories.

excused by one rabbinic passage is acknowledged by another (ch. 2(A): Josh. 6:17 and ch. 6: Deut. 12:5). In both instances the passage denying wrongdoing derives from classical rabbinic literature, whereas the passage acknowledging wrongdoing derives from rabbinic literature which post-dates the Babylonian Talmud. This trend of finding fault in the actions of righteous biblical characters continued into the works of the Medieval authorities, especially those of Ramban and Radak.[195]

Targum Jonathan was found to be quite useful in this study for resolutions in the first three categories, especially when no other solution could be found. Going beyond the realm of this study, it can be shown that Targum also

---

195. See Ramban, Gen. 12:10 and Radak, Gen. 16:6. It is a worthy task to make an exhaustive study of the cases in which Ramban and Radak acknowledge violations on the parts of biblical characters especially in Genesis. Before Ramban and Radak, the patriarchs and matriarchs were largely unblemished in rabbinic literature. *Tanna de-Vei Eliyyahu* 25 exhorts us to evaluate our own deeds to be in concert with that of our patriarchs. *Bereshit Rabbah* 40:8 has God telling Abraham to forge a path with his actions, for his descendants to follow. This is known as *ma'aseh avot siman la-banim*. The actions of the patriarchs serve as omens for their descendants. In this backdrop, it may seem preferable to explain every action of our ancestors in as good a light as possible insofar as they bear upon what will happen to us. And even though our Sages considered our patriarchs to be a direct conduit to God (*ha-avot hen hen ha-merkavah*, "the patriarchs are the chariot" — *Bereshit Rabbah* 47:8), there are quite a few midrashic and talmudic sources which called our patriarchs to task. *Bereshit Rabbah* (41:11) at first criticizes Abraham for not drawing Lot closer to his inner circle, while another opinion takes him to task for doing so! *Midrash ha-Gadol* 39:10 calls out Abraham for too readily agreeing to take Hagar as a wife, while *Tanhuma*, Shemot, criticizes Abraham for not properly disciplining Ishmael. In one place *Bereshit Rabbah* criticizes Abraham for making peace with the Philistines (54:5), while in another place criticizes Isaac for allowing himself to be duped by Esau (65:3). *Bereshit Rabbah* 67:4 is critical of Jacob's subterfuge regarding the birthright and later on (71:10) takes Jacob to task for his harsh conversation with Rachel. *Bereshit Rabbah* 75:6 considers that Jacob's abject fear of Esau was a breach of faith, and elsewhere (79:9) criticizes Jacob for refusing to consider Dinah as a wife for Esau, and even (84:8) finds fault with Jacob for his favoritism of Joseph. This is not an exhaustive list, but it does underscore that the Rabbis took a realistic and sometimes critical approach to the actions of our patriarchs and matriarchs.

resolved apparent violations of rabbinic law in Scripture.[196] Perhaps a study such as this can be expanded to include the treatment of Targum and other rabbinic literature to violations of rabbinic law in Scripture.

A significant phenomenon was discovered while observing the resolutions in Targum. Whenever there is a parallel passage in Chronicles to a violation in Samuel the version in Chronicles is often changed in order to resolve or explain away the violation. This phenomenon is well known. However, the significant fact is that Targum's rendition of some of the verses in Samuel cited in this study, is often an exact Aramaic rendition of the verse in Chronicles. For example, David violates the Torah by wearing a linen ephod (II Sam. 6:14; see ch. 15: II Sam. 6:14), The parallel passage in I Chron. 15:27 replaces *ephod bad*, "linen ephod," with *me'il butz*, "a robe of fine linen." Targum's rendition of *kardut de-butz* in II Sam. 6:14 is a direct translation of *me'il butz*.[197] Thus we see that Targum was aware of the desire of the Chronicler to resolve violations, and so followed suit. It also shows that biblical authors themselves were interested in resolving violations in the Bible.

The resolution of *hora'at sha'ah* is only mentioned in this study with reference to sacrifice (see ch. 8) and to David's treatment of Saul's seven descendants at II Sam. 21 (Chapter 35). It is significant that one of the sources is Tannaitic, because the concept of *hora'at sha'ah* is relatively unknown in Tannaitic literature.[198] The Rabbis reserved this resolution for the righteous. Rabbinic traditions do not relate any act of *hora'at sha'ah* performed by Achan or Ahithophel. Rather, the biblical characters to whom this category of resolution is applied include Gideon, Samuel, David and Elijah.[199] Also this resolution seems to be reserved for leaders.[200]

---

196. See L. Smolar and M. Aberbach's Studies in Targum Jonathan to the Prophets. A large selection is dedicated to Targum Jonathan's treatment of biblical as well as rabbinic law. See pp. 1-61.
197. See other such examples, Ibid. pp. 13-18.
198. The only other Tannaitic source which mentions *hora'at sha'ah* is Mishnah, *Parah* 7:6.
199. These four are generally viewed positively in midrashic literature.
200. See introduction, note 7.

The two sources cited earlier (Chajes and *Encyclopedia Talmudit*) which deal with *hora'at sha'ah* explain the various regulations and opinions regarding this principle.

The fourth category of resolutions of this study acknowledges violations of the Torah law, despite the fact that the biblical text seems to be unaware that a violation of the Torah law has taken place. For the purposes of this study it is not enough to record the fact that the Rabbis acknowledge the biblical character's guilt. If the person is indeed guilty, why didn't the biblical author note the fact? The fact that the Rabbis saw a violation is not proof that the biblical author saw a violation. The Rabbis, thus, read their awareness into the text by demonstrating in each of these cases that there is indeed an indication of violation in the biblical text. Of course none of these violations are explicitly noted in the biblical text. If so they wouldn't be included in this study. Nonetheless, a punishment embedded in the narrative is often sought in order to show that the narrator is indeed aware of wrongdoing.[201]

For instance the Rabbis acknowledge Jephthah's guilt for killing his daughter, beyond the silence of the biblical text regarding that action. According to the Rabbis, Jephthah is punished in the biblical text by being buried "in the cities of Gilead" (Judg. 12:7). For killing his daughter, limb after limb fell off his body and he was buried in many cities. This is by no means the plain meaning of the verse, and the fact that Jephthah was buried "in the cities of Gilead" is amply explained in post-rabbinic sources (see Radak and Ralbag, Judg. 12:7). Yet the rabbinic declaration of punishment is significant. It demonstrates how much the Rabbis tried to show that the text itself was aware of the violation, even in the absence of an explicit or implicit indication of the violation (see ch. 10).

---

201. These violations are considered to be in a different category than those in Judges 17-21. While the violations in these chapters are implied by the text, the punishment is alluded to in this category are not presented in the text as a direct result of the violations.

Another example of rabbinic acknowledgement of a violation involves David seeking the peace of Ammon (II Sam. 10:2), in violation of the Torah (Deut. 23:7). The Rabbis find punishment of this violation in the shameful way David's messengers were treated (II Sam. 10:4). David subsequently went to war with the Ammonites as a result of this disgrace. It was during this war that David sinned with Bath-sheba, an event that haunted the rest of David's life. In this example, the Rabbis have a concrete textual basis for saying that David was punished directly for his actions, in contrast to the punishment listed in the previous example regarding Jephthah (see ch. 30).[202]

---

202. It has been stressed that when the Rabbis acknowledged violation they searched the text for some hint at a punishment for that violation. This is the rule for this category except in the following case: The Rabbis seem to admit that Jonathan son of Saul violated the prohibition against divination (Lev. 19:26, I Sam. 14:8-10). However, the Rabbis make no mention of the punishment meted out to Jonathan. Moreover, it seems that Jonathan was rewarded with a stunning victory as a direct result of his apparent sin (I Sam. 14:12-14). Because of this, many post-rabbinic commentaries absolved Jonathan of sin (see ch. 19 note 98). In all cases in this category post-rabbinic sources can be found which absolve the alleged perpetrators of sin. However, this last example is unique because some post-rabbinic sources explain that the talmudic passage itself never meant to accuse Jonathan of sinning. In the previously cited example the Rabbis admitted that David sinned in seeking peace with Ammon. Nonetheless, post-rabbinic literature abounds with Rabbis who absolved David of sin (see ch. 30 note 144). Obviously these rabbinic opinions were not in agreement with the midrashic source which admitted David's guilt. The midrashic source acknowledging David's guilt is *Tanhuma*, Pinhas 3. This is in opposition to the talmudic claim that David never sinned (BT *Shabbat* 56a). Therefore it is not surprising that the Medieval authorities rejected the passage in *Tanhuma*. See however, Rambam, *Hilkhot Melakhim* 6:6 and *Kesef Mishneh* there. *Kesef Mishneh* cites Rabbi Eliezer of Metz, *Yereim* §250, that the Torah only prohibits *seeking* the peace of Amon. Returning a peaceful gesture on their part is permitted. *Yereim* cites David's actions favorably, and *Kesef Mishneh* responds: "This [exoneration of David] is curious, because the Sages in the Midrash [*Tanhuma*, Pinhas] have said that David acted improperly in this case [by sending peace to Ammon]." Indeed, the aforementioned Midrash in typical fashion finds punishment in the text in the very next chapter, which is the story of Bath-sheba. David's gesture of peace led to war with the Ammonites and it was during this war, while Uriah was at battle, that the Bath-sheba story took place. The Medieval authorities viewed Jonathan's case differently, perhaps because no punishment is sought by the Rabbis as a reaction to Jonathan's sin and the Bible itself seems to record the event favorably.

The fifth category of resolution acknowledges the violation but excuses it. The difference between this category and the first three is that in the first three the violation *is* without question denied. Of the 59 resolutions cited in the first three categories of resolutions, only one has a parallel passage in rabbinic literature which acknowledges a violation (see ch. 2). Every example cited in the fifth category, however, has a parallel passage in rabbinic literature which acknowledges the same violation without excusing it. Thus, this category does not emphatically deny sin, yet it explains why the biblical author does not note the sinful nature of the act.

The sixth category lists those violations which are not addressed in rabbinic literature. There are instances under this category, however, where the fact that a violation was ignored does not necessarily imply that the Rabbis were unaware of the violation, or that they had no resolution. For instance, Judges 17-21 includes many violations which seem to go unnoticed by the narrator, such as the making of a graven image (Judg. 17:3) in violation of Torah (Exod. 20:4). However, even though the narrator does not explicitly denounce these as violations of the Torah, they are nonetheless hinted at. The text in these three chapters stresses three times that in those days there was no king in Israel; everyone did as they pleased, Thus there was no need for the narrator to specifically denounce each act of wrongdoing in those chapters, and thus no need for the rabbis to resolve or acknowledge the violation.

In other instances, rabbinic silence is difficult to explain. If they considered a person guilty of a violation, why didn't they say so? And if they had a resolution why didn't they offer one?[203] This is the common question

203. Needless to say, rabbinic resolutions may exist that have eluded this researcher. The following example illustrates how I went about researching rabbinic resolutions for chapter 24, "Violations in Possessing a Graven Image," regarding the teraphim in David's house, I Sam. 19:13.
(a) *Torah ha-Ketuvah ve-ha-Masorah* [Hebrew], A. Hyman, All Torah verses which prohibit idols; I Sam 19:13; and all reference to teraphim in the Bible.
(b) "teraphim": in all major Hebrew and English Jewish encyclopedias, and a full Google search, of teraphim.

which links the violations in this category. Post-rabbinic resolutions are offered in all such instances.

Violations

The Rabbis offer resolutions for a failure on the parts of biblical figures to perform positive commandments. This is understandable. It is much easier to excuse failure to perform a positive commandment than to excuse a violation of a negative commandment.

The list of perpetrators under the heading "Violations Intended Which Were Never Actually Committed" is comprised of members of nobility (Saul, David, Tamar).[204] It seems that members of nobility are sometimes prone to use their position to go beyond the letter of the law in certain instances.[205]

Violations of the laws of sacrifice are all resolved in one of two ways. The Rabbis at times justify the apparent violation as an act of hora'at sha'ah or they indicate that the sacrifice which was offered outside the precincts of the Tent of Meeting was done so in accordance with the law at that time (see ch. 8).

The most extensive category involves the unlawful taking of a life. All these violations but two are either denied or explained away (see ch. 10, 24). One might have thought that the Rabbis would treat such severe violations

(c) *Otzar ha*-Aggadah [Hebrew], M.D. Gross, under the headings of *Avodah Zarah* and *David.*

(d) *Be-Netivot ha-Midrash* [Hebrew], H. Kuperman, under the headings *Avodah Zarah, David,* and *Mikhal.*

(e) *Ishi ha-Tanakh* [Hebrew], Y. Hasida, under the headings *David* and *Mikhal.*

(f) *The Conciliator,* on I Sam. 19:13.

(g) All Targumim, Medieval, and modern Jewish commentary to I Sam. 19:13 who may quote rabbinic literature on the topic, through computerized searches.

204. Samuel is also listed under this category (ch. 41) but is not included because his was of *hora'at sha'ah* by Divine decree.

205. See introduction, note 9. One has to wonder if Solomon's action in I Kings 3:25 falls under this category.

more harshly, yet this is not the case. The. majority of the resolutions of this category of criticism explain that the perpetrator exercised his special right as king in his actions (ch. 20, 21, 24, 27, 28, 33, 34, 36).

Violations of ritual laws are all resolved except one. Jonathan's violation of the law prohibiting divination seems to be acknowledged by the Rabbis (ch. 19). Most commentaries agree though, that the Talmud did not intend to condemn Jonathan's actions (see ch. 19, note 98; above note 202). With this understanding, we see that the Rabbis were intent on resolving violations of ritual law. This is not so regarding violations of the laws prohibiting idolatry. In fact, of the three instances in this study of violations of the law of idolatry (ch. 1, 14, 23), none are even addressed by the Rabbis! Violators of these laws include figures no less righteous than Joshua and David, yet the Rabbis are silent on these issues.

This study reveals that the common perpetrator of Torah violations in the book of Joshua, Judges, and Samuel is David (This is not to mention those Torah violations of his which are acknowledged by the text). In contrast, Saul's violations are few indeed. Rabbinic (and post-Rabbinic) sources abound which allow David the liberty of exercising his special rights as king, even the right to take the lives of his subjects when he saw fit. David did this on numerous occasions. Saul, on the other hand, is treated very harshly in midrashic literature, especially for his treatment of the priests of Nob. This is understandable. Yet the Rabbis could have ruled that Ahimelech was *mored be-malkhut* (rebelled) against Saul (see II Sam. 21:2-10) at least as much as Uriah was *mored be-malkhut* (II Sam. 11:7-13; BT *Shabbat* 56a). Rabbinic favoritism for David over Saul was sensed by the Rabbis themselves (see BT *Yoma* 22b). This kind of favoritism is found often in rabbinic literature.[206]

The Rabbis acknowledge the violation of a wide range of biblical characters whose violations go unnoticed in the text. Such illustrious figures

---

206. An important book which deals with rabbinic favoritism is E. Margoliyot's *ha-Hayyavim b'Mikra ve-Zakkaim b'Talmud u-v'Midrashim* [Hebrew].

as Joshua, Jephthah, Jonathan, and David appear on the list. In fact, no violations of wicked Israelites, whose violations go unnoticed in the text, are acknowledged by the Rabbis. A glance at the list of perpetrators of the entire study reveals that of everyone on that list, perhaps only Ahithophel (ch. 13) is considered wicked in the eyes of the Rabbis.[207] It is noteworthy that the Bible doesn't fail to record the sins of the wicked. The Bible's subjectivity in the way it records the actions of the righteous and the actions of the wicked can be seen from the way suicides in ch. 13 are recorded. (See also Zimri's apparent suicide in I Kings 16:18.)[208] One feels that the author applauds the suicides of Samson, Saul, and even Saul's armor-bearer. Yet one doesn't feel this way when reading of the suicide of Ahithophel. All of the suicides feared imminent death,[209] yet their stories are reported differently. It seems that the suicides of Samson, Saul, and Saul's armor-bearer are reported from their own standpoint. Ahithophel's suicide, on the other hand, seems to be reported from an outside perspective. He played an important role in an unsuccessful rebellion against David. Fearing sure death for rebelling, he took his own life.[210] The Bible, in recording Ahithophel's suicide, seems to ignore this fact (II Sam. 17:23).

The report of a biblical hero's actions in rabbinic literature seems to be colored by the nature of his character. Even in instances in which the biblical text condemns the righteous character for his actions, the Rabbis often offer absolution.[211] This favoritism was seen above in the rabbinic treatment of David and Saul. It is also evident on a large scale in the

---

207. See Mishnah, *Sanhedrin* 11:1.
208. So Abravanel. See however, Radak, I Kings 16:18.
209. Ahithophel played an important role in an unsuccessful rebellion against David. Fearing certain death for rebelling, he took his own life. Samson, Saul, and Saul's armor-bearer feared certain death at the hands of the Philistines.
210. See Radak, Ralbag, Abravanel, II Sam. 17:23.
211. See especially BT *Shabbat* 56a-b. In this passage, characters who in their totality are viewed as wicked by the biblical text (e.g., Eli's sons, Samuel's sons) are offered absolution for sin. See E. Margoliyot's *ha-Hayyavim b'Mikra ve-Zakkaim b'Talmud u-v'Midrashim* [Hebrew], Introduction.

following case. Chapter l(c) records seven different tribes who sinned by not destroying the Canaanites. Yet, only the sin of the tribe of Judah is resolved in Rabbinic literature. The sin of the other tribes in allowing Canaanites to reside amongst them is not addressed at all by the Rabbis. The preferential treatment afforded the tribe of Judah in the Bible influenced the Rabbis as well. This study has attempted to underscore this phenomenon in a variety of ways. The Rabbis treated biblical characters in different ways, often based on their understanding of how the Bible itself depicted a specific biblical figure.

It is fitting to close this study with an excerpt from Radak's commentary to I Kings 3:3, regarding Solomon's marriage to the daughter of Pharaoh:

> Solomon must have converted the daughter of Pharaoh. But even so, she was forbidden to him because she was an Egyptian of the first generation (the Torah only allows an Egyptian of the third generation to marry an Israelite — Deut. 23:8-9). Yet there are some Rabbis who claim she was permitted to marry Solomon because the Torah only excluded Egyptian sons, not daughters from joining the ranks of Israel immediately.[212]

Even though this opinion was not accepted halakhically, Radak considers it to be historically true.

Radak is so concerned about absolving Solomon of sin that he does so even at the expense of a halakhic ruling.[213] Yet a close look at the plain sense of I Kings 3:1-3 seems to indicate that Solomon did not violate the Torah law in his marriage to Pharaoh's daughter. Verse 1 indicates that Solomon married Pharaoh's daughter. Verse 2 indicates that the Israelites offered sacrifices at *bamot*. Verse 3 relates that Solomon walked in all the ways of God except for the sacrifices at the *bamot*. The juxtaposition of

---

212. This is the opinion of Rabbi Simeon bar Yohai, BT *Yevamot* 76 a-b.
213. See Rambam, *Hilkhot Issurei Bi'ah* 12:19.

these verses implies that the text disapproves only of the sacrifices at the *bamot*. Perhaps this was one of the motivating factors in the rabbinic ruling which allowed female Egyptian converts of the first and second generation to marry an Israelite. Here again we see how the Rabbis took their cue from a close reading of the biblical text itself. What we would categorize as a "violation unnoticed" by the biblical author did not go unnoticed by the Rabbis. In their own imaginative way, they explained why there was no violation to be noticed.

www.ingramcontent.com/pod-product-compliance
Lightning Source LLC
Chambersburg PA
CBHW021335090426
42742CB00008B/619